SY 0019896 X

ST. MARY'S
COLLEGE OF EDUCATION
LIBRARY
942.08/046

BAG

1574

ST. MARY'S COLLEGE OF EDUCATION

DATE BORROWED

BOOKS TO BE RETURNED ONE WEEK FROM DATE

-9. FEB. 1972 ✓

12. SEP. 1972 ✓

~~629~~

-7. FEB. 1975 ✓

29. OCT. 1976 ✓

~~28. OCT. 1978~~

24. NOV.. 83 R

D1421338

LIFE IN
MEDIEVAL ENGLAND

By the same author

UPHOLLAND GRAMMAR SCHOOL
The evolution of a school through three centuries

MARGARET OF ANJOU, QUEEN OF ENGLAND

A HISTORY OF LANCASHIRE WITH
MAPS AND PICTURES

HENRY VIII

The Gateway, Battle Abbey, Sussex

William I founded this Benedictine monastery on the site of the battle of Hastings as a daughter house of the abbey of Marmoutier, near Tours in the Loire valley. This magnificent gateway was built in the mid-fourteenth century

Life in
MEDIEVAL
ENGLAND

J. J. BAGLEY

English Life Series

Edited by PETER QUENNELL

LONDON: B. T. BATSFORD LTD
NEW YORK: G. P. PUTNAM'S SONS

1574

First published 1960
Third impression, 1962

REFERENCE LIBRARY

———o———

ST. MARY'S TRAINING COLLEGE
BELFAST

Section......*History*..................

| 942 | 02/046 |

© J. J. Bagley, 1960

Made and printed in Great Britain
by William Clowes and Sons, Limited, London and Beccles
for the publishers

B. T. BATSFORD LTD
4 Fitzhardinge Street, Portman Square, London, W.1

G. P. PUTNAM'S SONS
200 Madison Avenue, New York 16, N.Y.

Preface

Since most people tend to look back along the years from the viewpoint of the present day, there is a natural inclination for the more distant centuries to diminish in size and eventually to telescope into one another. Many, who are well aware of the vital differences in English life before and after the First World War or between the eighteenth and the nineteenth centuries, will often speak of the Middle Ages as a unit, as if life in Norman England differed very little from life in Yorkist England. But it is equally false to assume that the Middle Ages witnessed a steady uninterrupted improvement in living standards, and that progress was achieved by the members of each generation becoming slightly more enlightened than their parents. The truth was far more complicated than that. In some ways the twelfth century was more advanced than the fourteenth, in other ways the fifteenth century more depressing than the eleventh.

Just about as many years separated the battle of Hastings from the battle of Bosworth as divided Henry VII's accession from the beginning of our own century. During that long period of time, if we must accept the two battles as the arbitrary limits of the Middle Ages, twenty generations of Englishmen lived out their lives on this island. In a composite of word and picture this book attempts to sketch the varying backgrounds of those millions of lives, and to give the reader a general impression of what it was like to live in castle, village, town, or monastery during the different centuries of medieval times. It is a book based on the detailed work of other historians, but itself is a wide survey and not a close examination of a limited period or special topic. If the reader wishes to study further a particular aspect of medieval life, he is advised to go first to the list of books given at the end of each chapter.

ST. MARY'S TRAINING COLLEGE
BELFAST.

Apart from the many scholars whose books I have read so eagerly and acknowledged, alas, so briefly, I am particularly indebted to three people. My colleague, Dr. A. R. Myers, initially encouraged me to write the book, and has helpfully criticised each chapter as it has been written. By her forthright comments on the rough draft, Miss Joan Beck, honorary secretary of the Historic Society of Lancashire and Cheshire, has kept the needs of the general reader foremost in my mind, and my wife, as on previous occasions, has helped me in so many ways to finish the task in the agreed time.

University of Liverpool J. J. B.
March 1959

Contents

Acknowledgment

The Author and Publishers wish to thank the following for permission to reproduce the illustrations appearing in this book: His Grace the Archbishop of Canterbury and the Trustees of Lambeth Palace Library, for the illustration on page 147; Aerofilms Ltd., for page 24; G. Douglas Bolton, for pages 71 and 125; J. Allan Cash, F.R.P.S., for pages 132 and 139; the late Brian C. Clayton, for pages 4 (top), 5 and 141; the late F. H. Crossley and the Courtauld Institute of Art, for page 140; the late F. H. Crossley and the National Buildings Record, for page 74 (from *The Builder*); F. Frith & Co., for page 6; A. F. Kersting, F.R.P.S., for pages 3, 98, 101, 103, 104, 129, 134, 135 and 166; Liverpool Public Library, for pages 51 and 52; Eric de Maré, for page 49; the Museum of the History of Science, Oxford, for pages 110 and 111; the National Buildings Record, for pages 26 (top) and 94; Radio Times Hulton Picture Library, for pages 48, 146 and 149; Dr. J. K. St. Joseph, for pages 25, 30, 32 and 160; The Director of the Science Museum, South Kensington, for page 115; Edwin Smith, for pages 70, 75, 124, 136 and 138; the late Will F. Taylor, for page 79; the Dean of Wells Cathedral, for page 108.

The illustration on page 72 is from a print by Sutton Nicholls, 1720; on page 84 is a detail from a fresco by Giotto; and those on page 86 are from Dugdale's *Monasticon*, 1655.

The sources of the illuminated manuscripts, etc., are shown in the List of Illustrations.

List of Illustrations

I

Castle and Court

William of Normandy conquered England with no more than six thousand soldiers. The single victory of Hastings, won by the penetrative power of archers and the mobility of cavalry against the stationary defence of shields and battle-axes, gave him possession of London and the crown. His constables quickly mobilised labour to build castles at strategic points in the districts allotted to their particular care, for castles were the readiest and most effective means that the Normans had for preventing the English from revolting. Half the usefulness of a castle lay in its site. It must dominate a town, control the entrance to a harbour, or defend a river crossing. Nothing, therefore, was allowed to restrict the Normans' choice of position. At Norwich, Cambridge, and Lincoln, 98, 27, and 166 houses respectively were pulled down to make room for the castle. At Windsor 60 acres of agricultural land were earmarked for the site, and at Oxford it is probable that some of the 478 houses which Domesday Book described as *waste* were destroyed for castle building. By 1071 local resistance in the Midlands, East Anglia, and the northern parts of England had been so crushed or cowed, that William considered it safe enough to pay off and dismiss the mercenary soldiers who had been the rank and file of his conquering army. But that did not put an end to castle building. Domesday Book, written in 1086, records 49 castles built in the previous twenty years, and at least another 35 were built in England and Wales before the death of William Rufus in 1100.

None of these castles, with the notable exceptions of the

1

Tower of London and the castles at Colchester, Pevensey, and Chepstow, were built in stone before the next century, for permanent stone buildings would have taken far too long to erect for the Conqueror's immediate purpose. Speedy construction was essential, and so the Normans chose to build motte-and-bailey castles, a favourite form of defence in Normandy itself. As at York and Dover they could dragoon local, unskilled labour into building the motte, or mound of earth, in as little as eight days. A few days more were sufficient for defending the motte with a wooden stockade, and building

Normans attacking the motte-and-bailey castle at Dinan, Brittany. The attackers have bridged the moat dividing the bailey from the motte, and are trying to fire the wooden stockade

on its flat top the roughly-fashioned, stout, wooden shelters for the garrison. Meantime, below and across the moat, out of which most of the motte had been dug, other men could be setting up a strong fence round the bailey or ward, in which the garrison lived in normal times. The bailey could be defended, but was regarded as expendable. If the garrison troops were ever seriously pressed, they moved across the moat bridge, pulled it up behind them, and prepared for a long siege in the motte. The twelfth-century Norman castles, the remains of which can still be seen at Rochester, Carisbrooke, Appleby, Durham, and other places in England and Wales, are basically

Clifford's Tower, York: a fourteenth-century tower built upon one of the two mottes by which the Normans defended York against English attacks in 1068–9

motte-and-baileys built more permanently and elaborately in stone. The massive keep supplanted the motte, and, with its three or four storeys of basement for stores, entrance chamber, hall, and private apartments, provided the commander and the garrison with safer and more spacious accommodation. The new bailey, often divided by a turreted wall into outer and inner wards, was defended by a strong gateway and thick, high walls, mounted with towers at frequent intervals. All these Norman castles, both earth and stone, took full advantage of any natural defensive features which the site offered. A small, determined garrison could hold out for many months in such castles as William Peveril built on a steep limestone crag at Castleton in Derbyshire, or as Roger of Poitou built on the isolated hill, which rises sharply from the Ribble valley at Clitheroe in Lancashire.

Norman, Breton, and Fleming noblemen had been Duke William's chief supporters, though not necessarily on the field of battle, in the military venture of the Conquest. Once all resistance had been overcome, they looked for substantial rewards for their help. They were not disappointed. In a series of confiscations quickly following one upon another, the new king took possession of the lands of the English earls and thegns so completely that by 1086 only two sizable estates still remained in the hands of Englishmen. The king reserved to his own use about one-quarter of England: the rest he distributed among 170 or so of his most ardent supporters. William fitz

3

A Norman keep: Castle Hedingham, Essex, the home of the de Veres

Osbern became earl of Hereford; Odo of Bayeux earl of Kent; Robert de Comines earl of Northumbria; and Hugh of Avranches earl of Chester. Such powerful noblemen probably numbered up to 700 or 800 manors in their English estates; indeed D. C. Douglas has recently calculated that ten of them shared half the acres which William I granted to lay tenants. But at the other end of the scale there were tenants-in-chief, much more lowly in rank, who had been rewarded with a score of manors or even less.

Riches, great or small, were not given by the king without requiring something substantial in return, for William held that all land in England belonged to the crown. If the crown let or "alienated" land, the tenant, who was known as tenant-in-chief because he held directly from the king, was given use of the land in exchange for specified services. Estates thus granted were called fiefs or feuds, and were the essential framework of feudal administration. William demanded that his tenants-in-chief should give him advice when summoned to do so, should administer justice within their estates, and, more importantly, should raise and maintain their share of the 5,000 armed knights, which he required to be always available for garrison duty in the royal castles or for active service with the royal army. Neighbouring tenants were often made jointly

Attacking a castle wall with scaling ladders towards the end of the Middle Ages

responsible, by rota, for manning nearby royal castles. These duties, as well as the king's precaution of dispersing the lands of his most powerful tenants, compelled nobles to be continually travelling about the country.

Castles retained their military importance throughout the Middle Ages. Military engineers devised more damaging methods of attack. Sappers became skilled in undermining walls and gateways; assault parties equipped themselves with more flexible scaling ladders and heavier battering rams; assailants built taller siege towers, covered them with hides to protect them from hostile fire and brought them up to the castle ramparts under cover of a smoke screen; and ingenious inventors, using complicated systems of springs, thongs, twisted ropes and counterpoised weights, constructed siege-engines which could hurl heavy rocks and firebrands over the highest walls. Yet none of these mighty efforts and clever contrivances could alter the fact that even at the end of the Middle Ages it was easier to defend a well-built castle than attack it. To starve out the garrison remained the ultimate siege weapon, notwithstanding the uses to which gunpowder could be put from the fourteenth century onwards.

Neither kings nor barons, therefore, lost interest in their castles, but succeeding generations were liable to find that they became increasingly expensive to maintain and repair. Moreover, the more important castles had to be kept up-to-date, for improved methods of attack could only be nullified by new defensive designs. From the middle of the twelfth century

Caernarvon, a typical Edwardian castle

The Gateway of Harlech Castle. To imagine how it looked to an enemy, one must man the towers and arrow-slits with archers, and replace the present bridge and steps with raised drawbridge and heavy portcullis

masons were instructed to build keeps circular rather than rectangular, because defenders had found to their cost that it was difficult to cover and repel attacks made on the square corners of Norman keeps. But a century later it was considered best to abandon the keep altogether, and construct castles with two or three concentric defensive walls, with the hall, chapel, kitchen, and sleeping quarters of the garrison built on the inside of the curtain wall of the inmost bailey. The strength of these new castles lay in a series of high, projecting towers, fitted with spiral staircases and connected to each other both by outside ramparts and by enclosed passages running through the curtain wall. The towers were designed in such a way that the defenders on any one of them could fire upon assailants attacking neighbouring towers, and, with all the towers connected, it was possible to stage a less rigid defence than in a keep, and even to turn defence into attack. Edward I built castles of this pattern in north and south Wales. Beaumaris Castle in Anglesey, because the flatness of the site permitted it, probably approached nearest to the ideal theoretical design. After carefully choosing the sites of Caernarvon and Conway in order to make the best use of the Menai Straits and the river, Edward was content to use the town walls as his outside defences. He regarded the towns themselves as the outer baileys, and concentrated most of his defensive power in a single ring of connected towers round the inner baileys.

Gateways were given much more attention in later medieval castles. They were built taller, and fitted with such refinements as double drawbridges, iron-studded and iron-shod oak port-cullises which could be hauled up vertical stone grooves by a system of chains and pulleys assembled in a room above the gatehouse, arrow slits covering each stage of the entrance, and cunningly-placed holes in upper floors through which stones and fire could be dropped on the enemy. As at Denbigh and Harlech, some castles were designed so that flanking towers protected the approach to the gateway, and, as at Caerphilly and Warwick, some had barbicans built to serve the same purpose.

THE COURT

The medieval court was not fixed in one place. By definition it had to be where the king was, and he was nearly always inspecting his own scattered estates, visiting the castles of his more powerful tenants, or hunting. Rarely did the court stay more than a week in any one place. It aimed to move from castle to castle or from castle to hunting lodge, but its slow rate of progress and the distances to be covered often compelled it to pitch tents in the open for the night. There was no fixed sequence of visits, but William I established the tradition of holding feasts and conferences of his Great Council at Gloucester at Christmas, at Winchester at Easter, and at Westminster at Whitsuntide.

Careful planning was necessary in all this travelling because so many people were involved. The chancellor with his staff of priests and clerks was responsible for the safe-keeping of the chapel and all records and official papers. The steward looked after food supplies; the butler, wine and ale. Neither had light tasks, for when plenty was available medieval men and women ate and drank grossly. The king entrusted the care of his personal possessions, including his clothes, jewels and money, to his chamberlain and treasurer, and left his constable and marshal to provide for the numerous horses, dogs and hawks which travelled with the court, and also to command the impressive company of men-at-arms, which was necessary to

7

ST. MARY'S TRAINING COLLEGE
BELFAST.

safeguard the cumbersome and slow progress. These major court officials always required a large staff to help them, and by the twelfth century they were far too rich and dignified to do any menial duties themselves except ceremonially on special occasions. They were well paid, the chancellor especially so. An account of the king's household, *Constitutio Domus Regis*, written about 1135, shows that the chancellor was then receiving 5s. a day together with a best loaf, a supply of salt, generous quantities of best and ordinary wines, and a large wax candle and forty candle ends. The other major officials only received such remuneration if they did not have their meals with the

Part of a baggage train: luggage too heavy for pack-horses had to be carried by cart wherever the state of the roads permitted

household. If, as was usual, they depended upon the king for their meals, their daily wage was reduced to 3s. 6d., supplemented by two ordinary loaves, some ordinary wine, and the same supply of candles. Even this rate of pay was munificent when compared with the 1½d. a day received by the unskilled servants in the kitchens and the court-yard.

The baggage train of this roving court was a formidable sight. A long string of pack-horses carried tents, furniture, bedding, cooking utensils, personal luggage, and stocks of food. Even the royal chapel, with its relics and its candles carefully guarded by the chaplain, jogged its way along in this royal cavalcade on the backs of a couple of horses. Those who packed and unpacked the train acquired the skilled routine of modern circus hands, but only at a heavy expense of manpower were the royal family and the nobles who travelled with the king spared as much personal inconvenience and discomfort as possible. Even for them such journeys made at all times of the year were very exacting; for the scores of servants, whose incessant manual work alone made this type of life possible, there was no comfort and only the briefest pleasures.

At court privacy yielded permanent place to communal living. The king himself rarely expected to find it outside the tapestried hangings of his feather bed, for once the daily routine began, he was as much in the hands of other people as they were in his. Dressing, washing, and preparing the very occasional bath for the king were the duties of the king's tailor and ewerer. Cooking and dining normally required the work of many servants, for all who lived at court had to be fed, from the nobles who ate with their fingers at the king's table to the scullions who snatched and bolted what food they could in the corner of the kitchens. On festival occasions, the royal kitchens provided elaborate meals for hundreds of people. The butler ordered casks of wine, mead, cider and beer, and the steward ample supplies of beef, mutton, pork, poultry, and game of all sorts, from curlews to geese and from pigeons to peacocks. During the Christmas festivities of 1246, Henry III's court ate, in addition to other food supplies, 5,000 chickens, 1,100 partridges, hares, and rabbits, 10,000 eels, 36 swans, 54 peacocks and 90 boars; and when Richard II dined with his uncle, John of Gaunt, and the bishop of Durham in 1387, they required 120 sheep, 16 oxen, 152 pigs, 210 geese, nearly 900 hens and capons, 50 swans, 1,200 pigeons, quantities of rabbits and curlews, 11,000 eggs, 120 gallons of milk, and 12 gallons of cream to satisfy the hunger of their combined retinues. The king conducted the administrative business of the day occasionally in formal meetings of the Great Council, sometimes in informal consultation with some of his barons, but far more usually in private discussion with his chancellor, treasurer, or chamberlain. There were always petitioners to see, for the king was the source of justice and often heard and decided cases himself. But once business was over, the king turned to relaxation, either conversation with friends, or listening to minstrels, or feasting and drinking, or hunting, the sport which consumed

On medieval roads the horse-litter was far more comfortable than the solid-wheeled cart or waggon

so many of the leisure hours of the Conqueror, William Rufus, and Henry II.

This itinerant court had several disadvantages in addition to the discomfort which constant travelling and living out of

saddlebags imposed upon its
members. Its approach terrified
townsfolk and countryfolk alike,
for one never knew what demands it would make for food
supplies, or even for young men
and women to enter the royal
service. Its unpredictable move-

Dressing the king in his surcoat

ments made it difficult for petitioners and messengers to find
the king, and, as government tended to become more complicated, it imposed increasing burdens upon the royal officers
responsible for administration. In the chaos of the civil war
between Stephen and Matilda effective government of England
collapsed altogether, and when Henry II came to the throne
in 1154 he quickly discovered that, work and travel as hard
as he might, he could not reduce the mounting arrears of
legislative and judicial work which he alone was qualified to do.
The lands he had inherited stretched from the Scottish border
to the Pyrenees, and long absences from England were un-
avoidable. Moreover, he had inherited from the anarchy of
Stephen's reign such dangerous legacies as the unrestricted
building of baronial castles and the excessive recruiting of
armed retainers, two practices which threatened permanently
to reduce the authority of the crown.

To meet this new situation Henry made major administrative
changes. The first three Norman kings, following the Saxon
custom, had kept the royal treasure, coins, jewels, and rich
robes, partly in the king's chamber but mostly in the permanent
treasury at Winchester. It had been Henry I's custom at Easter
and Michaelmas to sit with his chief officers round the exchequer
board (a chess-board counting device on which to show the
illiterate the correctness of additions and subtractions) and
there receive and audit the accounts both of the minority of tax
and rent payers who paid directly to the king, and of the
sheriffs who collected from the counties. All money not immediately required was sent from these exchequer meetings to
Winchester. Henry II separated the exchequer from his wander-
ing court, established it in a permanent home in Westminster,

11

and authorised the justiciar to take charge of it during the king's frequent absences. Henceforward, the king was rarely present when the sheriffs came to the exchequer or when disputes concerning payments were settled in the exchequer court, and before the end of the century the logical step was taken of transferring the treasury from Winchester to Westminster. Similarly Henry II made freer use of Henry I's system of itinerant justices, by which accredited representatives of the crown, later to be known as king's judges, visited convenient centres to hear both criminal and civil cases, and to give judgments as binding and as authoritative as those given by the king himself in his own court. These changes made the administration more stable and predictable, and the long absence of Richard I on his crusading adventures allowed the justiciar and the judges to establish firmly their new authority and independence. The heaviest administrative burden now fell upon the chancellor and his staff, because they had still to be in constant touch with the king despite increasing work, an ever-growing mass of records, and the need for occasional consultations with the exchequer. To keep the work going as smoothly as possible the chancery resorted to various temporary measures until 1265, when the logical step was taken of giving it a permanent home in London—in Chancery Lane.

Whatever advantages a fixed and automatic administration might have for the officials and the public, from the king's point of view it was apt to give too much independence to his chief officers. It certainly raised the question of who directed policy, the king or the justiciar and chancellor. The young Henry III did not always manage to uphold his royal authority against the will of such powerful and experienced administrators as Ralph Neville, his chancellor, and Hubert de Burgh, his

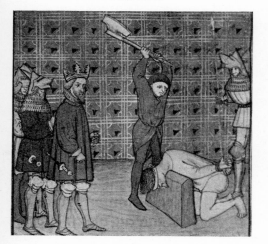

The king, the source of all justice, witnesses an execution

father's and his own justiciar, and he found it expedient to follow and develop his father's habit of entrusting as much work as possible to his household officials, the clerks of the wardrobe. In this way he kept a tighter rein on national government. He instructed his wardrobe clerks to seal important documents with the privy seal, which carried full royal authority, instead of using the great seal which was in the chancellor's care, and there is no doubt that wardrobe administration in the thirteenth and fourteenth century was far more supple and lively than the exchequer and chancery machines, which ran sluggishly because they were increasingly clogged with precedents and conventions. The king's use of the wardrobe did not offend the medieval conception of kingship. It was the king's duty to govern, and, though the barons claimed hereditary rights of advising the king, they would never admit that they were seeking to limit the crown's authority. Baronial criticism of John, Edward II, and Richard II was that they had misruled, not that they had ruled too vigorously. Consequently, until well after the Middle Ages, those ministers who were in the king's confidence, whatever their title might be, nearly always exercised the greatest power. The William Cecils and Thomas Wentworths of Tudor and Stuart times were spiritual descendants of such medieval royal officers as Peter des Rivaux and Robert Burnell. Peter des Rivaux, chief clerk of the wardrobe, helped Henry III to undermine the authority of Hubert de Burgh, and afterwards looked after the king's interests by serving as sheriff in no less than twenty-two counties. Robert Burnell, bishop of Bath and Wells, successfully combined the office of chancellor with the function of an intimate household adviser to Edward I.

THE TENANTS-IN-CHIEF

Those Normans who had received fiefs from William I had been obliged in their turn to alienate parts of their estates to others, in order to be able to fulfil their military obligations to the crown and provide themselves with sufficient armed retainers. Some tenants-in-chief were too openhanded. Dazzled by pride in soldiering and in commanding an impressive retinue, they did not appreciate the fundamental importance of

13

land, and, in three or four generations, when demesne farming was enriching well-endowed families, their descendants found themselves unable to hold their own even with some of their more thriving subtenants. On the other hand, other tenants-in-chief retained in their own control as much land as they could, and some of them, whose family fortunes were not blighted by unsuccessful rebellion or the succession of too many minors, succeeded in founding such powerful medieval families as the Beauchamps, Lacys, and Warennes. But very few of the major Norman families who started from scratch in 1066 were still among the leaders of society at the end of the Middle Ages. By the fifteenth century only the de Veres could claim unbroken descent in the male line from one of the Conqueror's companions-in-arms.

English medieval aristocratic society was not so unchanging as it sometimes appears to be. From the second half of the twelfth century, custom and law laid it down that, though the eldest son should succeed to all the estates of his father, the eldest daughter, were she left as heiress, should divide her inheritance equally with her sisters. On marriage all heiresses automatically transferred their lands to their husbands. The king had the feudal duty of seeing that unmarried heiresses of tenants-in-chief found suitable husbands, and heirs under age suitable guardians. He seldom had difficulty in fulfilling either duty, for eligible noblemen were only too willing to become suitors for the hand and the lands of a rich heiress, or even to compete for the guardianship of a minor when they were given the management and the profit of his estates until he came of age. To these natural hazards, which lay in the path of every family's progress, must be added political hazards. Additional grants of land, which were the usual reward for exceptional service and loyalty, and the confiscation of estates, which was the penalty for rebellion or, sometimes, for too steadfast a loyalty to an unfortunate king, frequently caused dramatic fluctuations in family fortunes. The Mowbrays of Northumberland, enfeoffed at the Conquest, had their estates confiscated for revolt in Rufus's reign, and the powerful earldom of Chester ceased to be independent in the middle of the thirteenth century when

14

Henry III, rather than let the inheritance be divided among co-heiresses, *distaffs* he called them, bought out all the rights of the nieces of the last earl, John the Scot, and annexed the fief to the crown. On the other hand few men rose so rapidly from comparatively humble beginnings to positions of great power

The high table in a noble's household

in the state as Hubert Walter in the reigns of Richard I and John, or Michael de la Pole in Richard II's days. And the remarkable story of the Holland family, which at the beginning of the thirteenth century held nothing more than a small freehold in Lancashire but which before the end of the fourteenth possessed the duchies of Exeter and Surrey and the earldoms of Kent and Huntingdon, shows what three or four profitable marriages and the patronage of such a powerful nobleman as Thomas, earl of Lancaster, could achieve.

Barons, who were the richer tenants-in-chief, were kings in their own domains. They built their own castles, employed their own sheriffs, held their own courts, and some of them had churches and monasteries which they regarded as their own possessions. They ran their households and estates in much the same way as the king did. They employed a chaplain to hold services and act as secretary of their households, a steward to manage their estates and supply their tables, and a chamberlain to be responsible for their wardrobes, personal effects, and money. To join these officers and their staffs at the common table there were the knights, the so-called bachelors, who lived permanently in the household, and other knights and squires who were doing their annual tour of duty with their lord. Baronial halls could be as crowded as the court itself, and round the baron's board sat down to dine as noisy and as exuberant, if not so distinguished, a body of fighting men as graced the royal table. Subjects of conversation and repetitive jest were fighting, hunting, horses and hawks, for this was essentially a military, sporting, open-air and physically vigorous society. Its heroes were warriors capable of exceptional daring, strength, and endurance. Normally it was good humoured, rough-tongued, and boisterous, but prolonged bad weather or any other factor which closed the natural outlet for its energy and emotion could make it moody, bad tempered, and dangerous. Even the princes of the Church were not outside this military, aristocratic society. As late as the fifteenth century the bishops of Carlisle and Durham, together with the abbots of the northern religious houses, were still expected to lead in person local resistance against the invading Scots.

THE KNIGHTS

The eleventh-century knight was little more than a housecarl, a professional soldier, often a foot-soldier, of low social rank who lived in a baron's household. But once the Conquest had been firmly established and it had become usual for barons and important subtenants to reward their knights with fiefs, the knight's social standing began to improve. He found himself a landowner with villeins and serfs of his own, and in return for these riches he gave forty days a year to military training or castle-guard, and, in time of war, served his feudal lord as a mounted soldier for at least two months at his own expense. A century after the Conquest a knight was usually expected to possess his own horses and armour, and to equip his armour-bearer, or, if he could afford to maintain one, his squire. Ideally a knight required at least three horses for his own use—a war-horse for fighting and jousting, a palfrey for normal riding, and a pack-horse to carry his luggage—but not until the thirteenth or fourteenth century can such opulence be considered normal.

A Christian knight

Necessary armour from the end of the twelfth century onwards included helmet, coat of mail, shield, and, later, greaves. It was best worn over gambesons, thick quilted under-garments, and it was so complete a covering that, long before plate armour replaced chain-mail in the fourteenth century, it would have been impossible to distinguish friend from foe but for the heraldic devices, usually simple in design and depicted in bold colours, which knights carried on their shields. Comparatively few knights were killed in battle, because the armour, the helmet apart, was strong enough to break a lance or resist a sword blow. But a well-aimed, powerful thrust with a lance could transform the spectacle of a fully-accoutred knight, charging fearsomely if ponderously into battle, into that of a bruised, half-conscious, helpless figure, often blinded by his rammed helmet, unable to rise from the ground without help, and ripe for capture and ransom. For aristocratic soldiers medieval warfare had some of the attributes of a game—a game that was played robustly, but gave good chances of survival even to the most regular players. Chaucer's fourteenth-century knight, who had come safely through fifteen "mortal batailles" in different

17

parts of Europe and Asia Minor, was not exceptional. Determination to win did not entail determination to kill. Ransoms were better rewards than dead knights, for not only might opponents be allies in the next campaign, but also knights throughout feudal Europe felt a greater affinity for one another than they did for the bowmen who fought at their side or the men who fed and groomed their horses. "Ransom-gambling chivalry" developed rather than diminished as the Middle Ages progressed.

The crusades gave fighting a noble purpose. The traditional,

Two Norman war-horses

vigorous life led by barons and knights could henceforward be enjoyed as a pious exercise, a penance, and a way to heaven. The crusading orders fostered the ideal of the Christian knight. The Templars and the Hospitallers came to England early in the twelfth century, and both Stephen and Henry II encouraged them to recruit knights for their orders, which were dedicated to be permanent scourges of the infidel. About the same time the troubadours of Provence began telling their stories of gallant knights performing endless feats of daring and honour in order to demonstrate the love they bore some noble lady, whose natural response was tragically, but not completely, curtailed by her married state or by vows of chastity. These popular stories engendered a romantic regard for beautiful and well-born ladies, if not for women in general, and the Church viewed with less than twentieth-century earnestness the perilous moral influence which such favourite stories as Abelard and Heloïse, Lancelot and Guinevere, and Tristram and Iseult might have on impressionable minds. It gave its blessing to this more kindly view of knightly purpose by adding the ceremony of the vigil to that of the dubbing of knights, by presenting each aspirant with his sword from the altar, and by encouraging the observance of a strict code of etiquette. Knightly honour existed before crusading orders or courts of

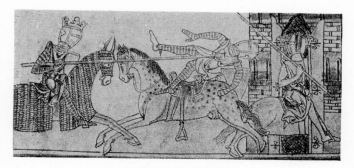

Unhorsed in the lists

love, but it was strengthened by these twelfth-century influences. Rarely did a knight break his parole, abuse the general peace of Christmas or Lent, or take his legal revenge upon a hapless hostage abandoned by a treaty-breaker. But his conduct usually fell far below the standards of the Knights of the Round Table, whose legendary exploits were written down by Chrétien of Troyes in the third quarter of the twelfth century, and sung all over western Europe by the minstrels. Sir Ector spoke better than he knew, when, with the words that Malory gave him in a fifteenth-century version of the stories, he said, "Sir Launcelot . . . thou wert never matched of earthly knight's hand; and thou wert the courteoust knight that ever bare shield . . . the goodliest person that ever came among press of knights . . . and the gentlest that ever ate in hall among ladies"; for in practice

19

the code of the medieval knight did not prevent him from sacking towns, killing non-combatants, despising and abusing women, and firing crops and villages when his blood was hot and the light of battle in his eye. And as in every age, there were the Bluntschlis, the chocolate-cream knights, who, in the words of Peter of Blois, loaded their pack-horses "not with steel but with wine, not with spears but cheeses, not with swords but wineskins, not with javelins but spits". Experience modified technique even in the Middle Ages.

Holders of knight's fees were not always able to fulfil their military obligations in their own person. As early as 1100 it was not unknown for knights to satisfy authority by paying an agreed sum, usually twenty shillings or two marks, so that the lord could engage another knight to do the necessary service. The payments were known as scutage or shield money. Many lords, including Henry II and his sons, preferred scutage to service, for the money could hire mercenaries, who lived for fighting and were ready to serve so long as they received regular wages. Without scutage it would have been difficult, if not impossible, for Henry II, Richard, or John to take armies across the Channel, but with the regular income which came from annual levies of scutage and aids, they could hire the services of knights at 8*d.* to 1*s.* a day, hobilars, or mounted infantry, at 4*d.*, and cross-bowmen at 2*d.*

A century later, armies raised upon the obligations of land-holding were tending to become things of the past. Many of the soldiers who served with Edward I and Edward II in Scotland and almost all who crossed the Channel with Edward III were indentured troops. Barons and influential knights known as bannerets agreed with the king to recruit, equip, train, and bring to the king's service squadrons of cavalry and companies of infantrymen. On his part the king undertook to pay regular wages, which he could only do by taxing the people. One of the reasons why thirteenth- and fourteenth-century kings periodically called together representatives of the shires and boroughs into the early parliaments was to make it easier and surer for the king to raise money.

THE BOWMEN

Norman commanders despised the foot-soldier. Many considered him fit only for guarding the stores during a battle, or for labour duties in camp. Nothing in their opinion could approach the effectiveness of heavily-armed cavalry. Richard and John, however, made good use of crossbowmen, whose bows were fixed to the end of a wooden stock, and who levered back their bow-strings mechanically and released their bolts with a trigger. But in English military circles crossbowmen were soon being equated with foreign mercenaries, and Magna Carta ordered them to be banished from the kingdom. The longbow gradually came into use in England in the thirteenth century, but not until Edward I's campaigns in Wales, where topography limited the effectiveness of heavy cavalry, did it acquire an honoured and well-established place in English arms. Welsh and English archers were used with startling results against the Scots at Falkirk in 1298. Later generations of English commanders so perfected the use of the longbow that in the major battles of the Hundred Years War, Crécy, Poitiers, and Agincourt, their combined use of bow and horse overwhelmed the French. At Crécy Edward III's 7,000 archers not only outshot the Genoese crossbowmen—they could shoot four or five arrows while the crossbowmen were firing one bolt —but they also prevented the massive squadrons of French cavalry from getting near enough to the English positions to turn the battle into a hand-to-hand struggle. Poitiers repeated the success of Crécy, and, despite the victories of du Guesclin in the long interval between 1356 and 1415, the power of the English archers again surprised the French at Agincourt. In the first movement of the battle they killed so many French horses that the constable of France could not prevent retreating

Longbowmen at the butts

Crossbowmen

men-at-arms from spreading fear and despondency through the whole of the French army. Shakespeare's list of the English dead,

> *Edward the Duke of York, the Earl of Suffolk,*
> *Sir Richard Ketley, Davy Gam esquire:*
> *None else of name; and, of all other men*
> *But five-and-twenty*

is exaggerated, but not outrageously so. English losses probably did not number more than a hundred, against French losses of about five thousand.

So great an impression did the longbow make upon English minds that even in the late sixteenth and early seventeenth centuries, when it had become outdated by gunpowder, the law insisted upon young men becoming proficient in its use. In a sermon before Edward VI, Hugh Latimer described the "Arte of Shootinge" as "a gift of God that he hath geve us to excell all other nations withall", and he deplored "that so excellent a gift . . . should be so little esteemed". The statutes of several Tudor and early Stuart grammar schools insisted upon pupils being regularly practised in the use of the bow, and justices of the peace were bidden see that the archers of the county militia did not allow their skill to rust. It was as nostalgic and pitiable a point of view as using cavalry against machine-guns, or retaining stirrup-pump and rifle training in days of rockets and megaton bombs.

Further Reading

The Oxford History of England, Vols. 3, 4 and 5.
Doris M. Stenton, *English Society in the Early Middle Ages.*
A. R. Myers, *England in the Late Middle Ages.*
Charles Oman, *A History of the Art of War in the Middle Ages.*
Sidney Toy, *The Castles of Great Britain.*

Manor House
and Peasant's Cottage

Farming dominated medieval economy. King, nobleman, merchant, cleric, and peasant were all so directly concerned with the growing of crops and the rearing of animals and poultry that none of them could afford to shrug his shoulders when unseasonable weather, plague, floods, or drought threatened agricultural disaster, for the well-being of all during the next twelve months hung on the success of the local harvest and the quality and quantity of fresh and salted meat. As daily he watched the progress of his crops and with trepidation looked for the first signs of sickness among his cows, sheep, pigs, and poultry, the medieval farmer's anxiety was greater than a modern farmer's, because he was more often concerned not with profits and losses but with the stark reality of survival or starvation. For safety's sake he followed the same daily and annual routine that his father and grandfathers had done before him, and that he was already teaching his sons. There was little room for experiment or variation. Not only was every farming community capable of compelling its members to toe the traditional line, but also no one could bear the loss which the failure of a major experiment would involve.

THE VILLAGE

English villages usually fall into one of two categories: the compact village with its houses gathered round a green or

ST. MARY'S TRAINING COLLEGE
BELFAST.

cross-roads; or the long-street village in which expansion has meant adding more houses at either end of the street. These patterns are often still visible where cities have not devoured the villages or industrial demands transformed them into busy towns. If the imaginative visitor shuts out from his mind's eye obvious nineteenth- and twentieth-century development, he can often still see the shape and estimate the extent of the medieval village which once stood there. Most probably the

Biddenden, Kent: a compact or nucleated village

old church, extensively repaired, enlarged, and occasionally improved by money collected on the authority of an eighteenth-century church brief or given by Victorian benefactors, still dominates the village centre, drawing all roads towards it, and compelling modern traffic either to crawl through the village bottle-neck or by-pass the village altogether. But the manor hall is not always to be found, sometimes because the stone-built successor to the wooden medieval hall has in turn been pulled down, and sometimes because the village never had one. Richer land-holders were lords of more than one manor. The king himself owned large groups of manors in different parts of England, and he and his tenants-in-chief managed many of their manors through bailiffs and reeves, who had no need for a house much bigger, or any bigger, than a freeman's cottage. Moreover the boundaries of village and manor did not always march together. Some manors contained several villages: other villages were divided between neighbouring manors. But the village was the real community. To all but the lawyers and the lord of the manor, the communal living of the villagers, working, rejoicing, and mourning together, was a greater reality than manorial rights and administration.

From what remains in an English village today, however, even the most imaginative visitor can gain no idea of medieval housing, because the building activity of the Tudors and early Stuarts swept away the cottages which had been patched up for scores of years, and built stone or brick cottages on the same sites. With very few exceptions, the oldest ordinary dwelling houses standing in English villages today date from no earlier

Stilton, Huntingdonshire: a long-street village

25

A cruck cottage, Didbrook, Gloucestershire. Auxiliary timbers pegged on the outside of the crucks made possible a wider roof-span

than the sixteenth century. Medieval cottages were dismal, depressing, unhealthy, foul-smelling, and short of head room. Many were home-made hovels built of clay and stone, and serving as common, one-room homes for man and wife, children and animals. Better cottages had a wooden framework knocked together by the village carpenter. Pairs of curved timbers, known as "crucks", were set up at either end to make two archways. These were joined together at the top by a heavy ridge pole, half-way down by purlins, and at the bottom by sills, and the whole "cage" or framework was strengthened by pegging shorter uprights and laterals to the main timbers by means of stout oak pins. A doorway and one or two small window-frames were put into position, and walls were made by tightly packing daub, a mixture of clay, dung, and straw, onto a frame of wattle laths. Where they were readily available, flints and pebble stones were set into the daub to give a different finish to the walls. Roofs were usually thatched with rye or wheat straw. Most houses were divided into two sections, hall and bower, used by some families as living-room and bedroom, by others as family home and stable. *Hall* implied nothing that was impressive or spacious, and *bower* little that was romantic or poetical.

The lord of the manor and the priest, if he had a good patron, might live in a wooden house built on stone foundations, but, apart from more room and surer protection from the weather, such

Taking a swarm of bees

a house offered no more amenities than the peasant's cottage. There was no better lighting in either than a wax candle or a tallow dip, both expensive to buy. Smoke from the fire, which burned in a clay-lined hole in the floor, had to find its curling and sooty way out of the narrow windows, doors and crevices of daub and timber houses alike. To both, water had to be carried from the river or village well, and for both sanitary arrangements were primitive earth closets or pits. The floors of both were the natural earth trodden or beaten hard, but in wet weather muddy and oozing water. Even those housewives who covered their floors with rushes renewed them so in-

Milking a newly-calved cow

frequently that they became unwholesome. Dampness encouraged decay, and the lack of ventilation from the small, shuttered, but rarely glazed windows made the atmosphere none the sweeter. Chaucer's *Nun's Priest's Tale* begins with a description of "a ful simple lyf" lived in "a narwe cotage", the home of a widow, three daughters, three large sows, three cows,

> *and eek a sheep that highte [was called] Malle,*
> *Ful sooty was hir bour, and eek hir halle.*

And William Langland in *Piers Ploughman* depicts a small cottage in which the housewife, harassed by "a crew of children", has to do all her work, spinning, washing, and caring for

27

the babies, in the restricted space of the one narrow room. In the richest village home, furniture was as scanty as in a camper's tent or a wartime barrack hut. A board supported on trestles or stumps of trees served as a table. The few stools, insufficient in number if all members of the family were in the house at the same time, and the wooden bowls, plates, and spoons were the reward of many winter-days' carving by the householder. The beds laid along the sides of the walls were straw pallets or bags of dried fern or heather. Both adults and children slept in their day clothes, and most had to do without further covering. Little wonder that medieval man never tired of praising the merry

Butchering pigs—notice how lean and small medieval animals were

month of May as the merriest month in all the year "when softe bene the wedres [weather]" and "every feld is ful of flours". The prospect of four months of outdoor living was before him, and such winter hardships as dark evenings, long nights, and shivering day-breaks were far enough ahead to be temporarily forgotten.

Each villein and freeman built his cottage on his croft, a strip of land which in most villages ran from the rough, stony track, which was the village street, to the edge of the common field. No building line regimented the houses: villagers built to suit their fancy, and, instead of the uniformity of subtopia, they collectively tended to achieve the jumble of shanty town.

28

Every ounce of use was squeezed out of the croft. In the summer it was the kitchen garden producing onions, cabbages, beans, and peas, if the villager had seed and luck with the weather. Ordinary folk could not afford such imported spices as pepper and ginger, which were brought into England in increasing quantities as the Middle Ages progressed, but thrifty housewives contrived to grow parsley, leeks, garlic, sage, fennel and other herbs to garnish the stock pot. "Wel loved he garleek, oynons, and eek lekes", said Chaucer of the Summoner. These delicacies were doubly welcome when the meat in the soup was tainted, or when salted herrings, almost universal food in Lent, had jaded the palate. Like Grisilde in *The Clerk's Tale*, housewives gathered herbs in the woods to shred and to boil in the stew, and if at the same time they came across any wild honey, they deemed it a great prize, because honey was the only available means of sweetening. Fruit trees, apples, pears, and in appropriate areas cherries and plums, grew in the crofts, but their fruits were all smaller, harder and less sweet than modern fruits. In the autumn the croft housed the unthreshed grain, and was the place where the housewife brewed ale or made cider and perry when there was grain and fruit to spare. Richer households brewed ale any time during the year, but poorer people had to be content with an October brew, and drink buttermilk or water when the casks were empty. In the winter, sticks and logs were piled outside the house for fuel, and the rest of the croft sheltered such animals as the villager managed to maintain through the lean months. A handful of scraggy hens pecked and scratched in the croft for what they could find, and the family always derived comfort from the sound and smell of a pig or two, razor-backed though they might be, snorting around both outside and inside the house. Pigs ensured plenty of "coloppes" (bacon) to go with the eggs: empty crofts spelt starvation.

THE FIELDS

Separated from the back of the crofts by a narrow right of way was the nearest of the open fields. Most, but not all, English villages organised their farming communally in unenclosed fields, in which each family held allotted areas together with rights of pasture on the common. The lands of every family were very scattered, and father and sons wasted much time and energy getting from one patch of plough to the next. This apparently haphazard distribution was due partly to an innate sense of justice that each family should share distant and near, and good and poor land, and partly to the piecemeal carving of

Ridge and furrow still to be seen from the air at Soulbury, Buckinghamshire. The direction of the ridges was largely determined by draining requirements

new arable land out of the woodlands and waste which surrounded the village.

Domesday Book paints a picture of islands of cultivation and habitation set in a sea of trees, moors, moss, and scrub. In some areas such as the Midlands and East Anglia, the islands were crowded together, but in others, such as the North and Wales, there was considerably more "sea" than "land". Suffolk and Norfolk, with an average of about fifty people to the square mile, were the most crowded counties, but the distribution of the people was so uneven that large parts of the two counties had less than half that density. Yorkshire and the area covered by modern Lancashire had about 30,000 and 10,000 inhabitants respectively, and their population density could not have been more than a tenth of that in the south-eastern counties. Despite a high birth rate, increase of population was drastically controlled by high infant and child mortality and recurrent plague, so that between the Norman Conquest and the Black Death, a period of three hundred years, the number of people living in England struggled onwards from about two to about five millions. Slow though this increase was, it did mean that there were many more mouths to feed and backs to clothe, and obviously this could only be done if the expansion of cultivated land kept pace with the increase of village population.

Each generation made its contribution to this heavy task of reclaiming the nearest woodland and waste, and enlarging the open fields. When necessity compelled or favourable circumstances invited them to do so, groups of neighbours set about felling oak, ash, beech, and elm trees, digging out roots, burning bushes and grasses, levelling the ground, draining away standing water, or, in the fen areas of eastern and south-west England, driving back salt water and winning land from the sea. One, two, or several seasons later, according to the difficulty of the task and the time available for the work, a new "assart" or "furlong" was ready for cultivation, but, since it was the result of the hard work of many hands, it had to be divided into strips, known in different villages by such names as *lands*, *flats*, *shoots*, *intakes*, and *selions*, so that each family's labour could be rewarded. In the course of a century, if population increases made them necessary, a dozen such assarts could have been made on various sides of the village, and each family would have a dozen new selions to cultivate in different parts of the open fields.

Furlongs varied in length and area according to the terrain and local requirements, but most villagers liked selions to be the right size for a full day's ploughing. The best shape was a long strip of land about six to twelve or more yards wide running the whole length of the furlong. This meant less turning for the oxen that pulled the plough, less wasted land at the headlands, easier access to selions, and a fair distribution of fencing, because if each family fenced the head of all their strips which abutted on the cart-road, the whole of the open field would be inexpensively but adequately protected from straying cattle. A few narrow grass foot-paths or balks gave access to different parts of the fields, but in most open fields, especially

Laxton, Nottinghamshire, still farms open fields, but has consolidated the old narrow strips into rectangular holdings

in the Midlands, the Welsh marches, and the eastern half of the north-eastern counties, no better defined boundary between family holdings was necessary than the double furrow, which resulted from holders of neighbouring selions ploughing each side of the boundary line from opposite ends and turning the soil inwards towards the middle of their own land. This simple system of marking boundaries had the supreme merit of not wasting precious soil on pathways, or equally precious time and material on erecting fences. But it depended upon mutual trust, and inevitably manor courts were constantly hearing complaints about trespass, about the moving of boundary stones which the ploughmen used in sighting the line of their outside furrows, and about neighbours reaping where they had not sown. Ploughing round each selion from the outside to the centre tended to pile the soil into a central ridge running the whole length of the selion, and since the double-furrow boundary lines had always to be in the same place, every season's ploughing made the ridges more permanent. Where the soil was heavy and clayey, ridge and furrow or high-backed lands, as this method of ploughing was variously called, helped to drain it; where the soil was light and sandy, and moisture was precious, the ridge had to be deliberately ploughed out in the fallow season to prevent it from becoming permanent. Today aerial photographs can still show clearly the ridge and furrow pattern of fields that have either long been enclosed, or for generations used only as pasture.

A two-field system, in which land was cropped and fallowed in turn every year, was widespread in the early Middle Ages, and where land was plentiful or particularly infertile, the system never improved. Alternatively, an in-field, near the village and heavily manured, was ploughed regularly, and an out-field, normally used for pasture, was kept in reserve for extra cultivation when necessary. On the downs and wolds, sheep and corn were often rotated in a special kind of two-field system. But the usual number of cultivated open fields in medieval England was three. By common agreement the villagers sowed in one an autumn crop, usually rye, wheat, or a mixture of both, and in the second a spring crop, usually barley, oats, or beans. The third field they left fallow for the animals to roam over, cropping the weeds and dunging the land. Each year they moved the crops round in a regular, pre-ordained cycle, and fitted the rotation into an annual farming programme, which was maintained by successive generations as regularly as the weather and the health of the community permitted. No sooner had the corn and barley harvests been gathered than it was time to

ST. MARY'S TRAINING COLLEGE
BELFAST.

A simple wooden plough used in Norman England

plough the field that had been lying fallow all summer, and sow it with winter corn. Good ploughing days in winter were spent on the second field, which in March was sown with the spring crop. The new fallow field was usually given a late-spring ploughing, and then hay-making, cultivating crofts, caring for livestock, repairing and constructing buildings and fences filled the summer days until harvest time once again called out every possible helper into the fields.

Few parts of England and Wales were without some communal agriculture of this kind, where neighbours cultivated their strips side by side and followed a crop rotation together. In the wide acres of the midland counties from Wiltshire to Yorkshire and from Cambridgeshire to Gloucestershire, the three-field system was the regular pattern throughout the Middle Ages. But in other parts of England and Wales where mountain, moor, or marsh restricted the possible areas of cultivation, or, as in Essex and Kent, where economic organisation was in advance of the rest of the country, open fields had obvious drawbacks and tended to be limited both in area and duration. Assarts in less populated areas, such as central Wales, eastern Lancashire, and the Lake District, were often the work of a single family, and from the first these irregularly-shaped, small fields were hedged or fenced with earth banks and treated as single units. They were never divided between neighbours: they began life as enclosures privately owned. As clearance progressed and the number of enclosures increased, the strips in the open fields represented a smaller and smaller percentage of the cultivated land in the village, and there were early moves to group the strips together and convert them into private enclosures. Indeed the disappearance of communal agriculture seems to have been earliest both in the least populated parts of the country, where there was no pressure on space and some families had long lived in tiny scattered hamlets and single farmsteads, and in the most developed parts of England, where a money economy was most advanced, and it was possible and profitable to grow crops for sale in town markets, and not merely in order to keep food on the family table during the coming year.

Medieval man showed more skill in cultivating the land than he did in stock breeding. He improved his tools, particularly his plough, to which he added the coulter and an efficient mould-board. He learned the importance of crop-rotation, manuring, and marling. He displayed enthusiasm, energy, and determina-tion in clearing fresh ground, and even though he regarded a three-fold return as satisfactory, he occasionally experimented by sowing seeds more thickly than usual, and he was aware that it was better to get his seed corn from another village than to sow what he had saved from his own harvest. But throughout the Middle Ages the villagers' domestic animals were left to fend for themselves, despite the fact that they represented a high percentage of village resources. In the summer the animals lived on odd patches of grass on the waste and in the woods. After hay-making they were allowed into the meadows, and after harvest into the open fields where, fortunately for them, the reaping hook left a long stubble. In the winter and early spring they were confined to the closes, and lived on hay made on the family strip, or *dole*, in the common meadow, on bean-bines and chaff saved from harvesting and threshing, and on acorns, beech mast, and leaves gathered from the autumn woods. Pigs were easiest to rear because in the woodland they could find food for themselves during most of the last quarter

A much more efficient plough used in the fourteenth century

35

of the year, and consequently pork and bacon were the commonest meats to be found salted in a peasant's hut. Milk and wool were such valuable products that villagers could not afford to look upon cows and sheep primarily as sources of beef and mutton. It was better to put up with sinewy beef or tough mutton than to slaughter animals too early, and lose months of milk supply or two or three fleeces.

Yet towards the end of every summer, villein, freeman, and even lord of the manor had to calculate shrewdly how many animals he could hope to keep alive during the winter. A good hay harvest might reprieve an extra cow, or a plentiful supply of acorns a couple more pigs, but family needs had to be the chief consideration. The end of winter and the early weeks of spring were harassing times for humans as well as for animals. When stocks of salted meat, dried beans and peas had all been eaten, when the level in the flour bins was dangerously low, and when nothing of the new harvest was likely to be ready for weeks, then the peasant was particularly liable to defy the manor regulations, risk heavy fines in the manor court, and attempt to poach hares and rabbits in the woods, pigeons from the lord's dovecot, and fish and eels in the pond or river. He did not scorn to catch singing birds to eke out his scanty stores. At that time it was a double joy to have a pig for slaughtering, or an adequate supply of eggs, or spare milk for cheese-making, because any of these extra foods would help the family through the lean weeks until the first days of August, Lammas time, when the three months of comparative plenty began. In an oft-quoted passage, Piers the ploughman laments that he is short of food in the house, that he has only two "green", that is new, soft, cheeses, a few curds, an oaten cake, two loaves of beans and bran, some parsley, cabbages and leeks, a cow and calf, and a draught mare, but when Lammas time comes he hopes "to have harvest in my croft", and then he will be able to provide a dinner that he will be proud to offer to his guest.

THE DEMESNE

Notwithstanding communal farming, open fields, and interdependence, the medieval village was made up of families which

Reaping the corn harvest

differed widely in wealth and local prestige. The main division lay between the free and the servile families, but in each category there were wide variations. The freeholders acknowledged that they were tenants of the lord of the manor by paying a money rent, and, in some manors, by working on the demesne lands for a few days each year, or by giving the lord a fixed number of sheaves of corn or head of poultry at harvest or at Christmas. They claimed the right of appealing to the royal courts if they were in dispute with their lord, but very few attempted to exercise this right. Litigation was expensive and frightening to those who were new to it, and most lords had means of influencing the courts, where impartial justice could never be taken for granted. The unfree tenants, the villeins and serfs, did not possess this theoretical right of appeal. They were subject to the jurisdiction of the lord himself in the manor court,

Stacking the corn

37

and they were not free to move house, sell any stock, or even marry without the lord's permission. In most manors the unfree tenants paid for their land in labour and in kind, but in others, particularly those belonging to big estates, these traditional payments were early commuted into money rents. This made the buying and selling of land in villages all the easier, and certainly from the end of the twelfth century it is not possible to distinguish between free and servile by the area of land they farmed. Some villagers had full-time employment as hired labourers on the demesne lands, or as servants in the manor household: some spent most of each working week doing such skilled work as milling, thatching, and carpentry. At best these villagers could be only part-time farmers on their own account, and they lived mostly on the wages and payments in kind which they received from the lord for whom they worked, or from their fellow villagers for whom they carried out services. It was not unknown for villeins to hire other villagers to work for them on the family lands, and a generation of successful farming could increase considerably a family's holdings. The manor court rolls served as a registry for the buying and selling of strips and enclosures, and they often illustrate jealousy and rivalry between neighbouring families.

The lord of the manor, were he king, baron, knight, or abbot, had many privileges and rights. He could select a large area of the tilled and meadow land of the village for his own use. This demesne land could be

Carting the corn

enclosed or scattered in furlongs in the open fields, and its needs took precedence over the needs of the peasants' strips. The villeins and serfs had to leave their own sowing and harvesting if the reeve called them to work on the demesne, and the lord could order all the village cattle to be grazed on his fallow or grass land if he felt that the demesne required extra manuring. Where the lord did not exercise this right of farming part of the village himself, he rented an equivalent acreage to local freemen. He usually reserved the river fishing to himself, and even where the king's forest laws deprived him of deer-hunting, his rights of warren gave him full control over the trapping and hunting of other game. From

Harrowing and bird scaring

about 1200, richer lords who held suitable lands were increasingly inclined to enclose private parks for grazing deer and to mark out chases for hunting, but such extravagances the average lord of the manor could never afford. The demesne fishponds and large pigeon loft kept the manor-house table supplied throughout the year, and when they sat down in the manor hall at harvest home or one of the religious festivals which the lord traditionally celebrated with a feast for his tenants, the villagers got a partial return for the grain which flocks of manor pigeons had filched from their ripening crops. Many lords could afford to buy imported dried fruits and to keep good cellars of wines from France, the Holy Roman Empire, and the Levant. Fruits and wine got no further than the high table, but one of the compensations of being a manor servant was to be reasonably

*Bringing a sack of grain to be ground
at the lord's mill*

sure of having better and more ample food than that available in the cottages.

The lord of the manor built the mill, and required every villager to use it and pay the customary fee, usually one sixteenth of the flour which the grain yielded. Many villagers heartily disliked this monopoly, and, evidence or not, suspected their miller of cheating and, like Chaucer's miller, taking three times his due. They would have preferred to grind their corn painstakingly and primitively in a quern or hand-mill, rather than entrust it to the miller. They hated losing sight and temporary control of that which was so essential for their well-being during the next twelve months. But there is no doubt that the mill, one of the few forms of mechanical power used in medieval times, fully justified its place in village life. The earliest kind was the water mill, and in those parts of the country where there was little difficulty in maintaining a satisfactory head of water, this type of mill continued to give good service until centuries later it was replaced by steam-driven machinery. In drier and flatter counties, chiefly in east and south-east England, windmills were erected in increasing numbers from the end of the twelfth century. A massive central post, sunk into the ground or held securely in a platform of bricks or stones, formed the pivot upon which the mill could be swung by hand to bring the sails into the wind. It was as big and as expensive an engineering structure as a siege-tower, and none but the lord could afford to set it up in the manor. Once he had done so he felt morally as well as legally justified in insisting that everyone used it.

Village milling was only one of the capitalist enterprises which lords of the manor developed and organised partly with hired and partly with servile labour. Fishing and bird-catching were extensively carried out in the fen and marsh-land villages. In the Weald, North Riding, parts of the Midlands, and the Forest of Dean, iron mining and smelting grew into profitable industries, and other miners were employed digging out tin and silver from south-western estates, lead from hillsides in

A medieval water mill, with eel traps set in the mill-race

Cumberland, Derbyshire, and Somerset, and coal from an increasing number of shallow pits in the northern counties. In the chases on the Pennine slopes, such lords as the earls of Lancaster and the lords of Clitheroe owned cattle- and horse-breeding stations, which were so successful and long-lived that Drayton, a contemporary of Shakespeare, could comment that "there no such Cattell be, for largenesse, Horne and Haire as these of Lancashire." But easily the most wide-spread and profitable enterprise was sheep-farming. On the downs and the wolds and on the broad backs of the mountains in the north and west, thousands of sheep were grazed. Local peasants owned a few head each, but the big flocks belonged to the lords of the manor, ecclesiastical and lay, to whom went the main profits from the sale of wool.

The royal sport of deer hunting

41

The fashionable sport of hawking

THE FOREST

The royal forest restricted the freedom of peasant and lord alike. William I introduced the forest to England, by declaring that specified areas were to be reserved for the royal hunting and protected by stringent forest laws. Successive kings created new forests, so that, by the end of the twelfth century, forest officially covered about one third of England. Obviously these extensive hunting grounds could not be restricted to virgin woodlands or wild moorlands. They included such settled areas as large parts of Berkshire, Hampshire, Oxfordshire, Nottinghamshire, and Essex, and scores of well-established villages, with their open fields and meadows, found themselves overnight newly included "within the metes and bounds of the king's forests", and subject to the forest laws which the king's officers —foresters, wardens, and verderers—were appointed to enforce. The king's deer were sacred. To kill a deer unlawfully was just as serious as to kill a man. It was strictly forbidden to damage or reduce deer pasture, the vert, by tethering cows on it or by ploughing it up, and the forest law demanded that fences should be carefully maintained so that deer could not stray into places outside the protection of the law. Dogs had to be "lawed" by having the claws of their forefeet cut, so that they could not be used for hunting.

The forest laws were onerous from the beginning of Norman rule, but their weight was felt most heavily when necessity began to force villages to cultivate more land. There seemed no moral reason why men should tolerate laws which put the interests of deer before those of human beings, and the hero-worship of Robin Hood reflected widespread anger. Fortunately in their anxiety for money, Richard I and John were prepared to strike bargains. Surrey landholders paid Richard 200 marks to release a good stretch of their county from the forest. The men of Devon paid John 5,000 marks for similar privileges, and "the knights, thanes and free tenants dwelling in the forests of the Honour of Lancaster" gladly collected and gave him 700 pounds weight of silver, so that they would be allowed to cultivate their lands at will "without disturbance of the king's bailiffs". In three clauses of Magna Carta the barons forced John to promise to lighten the weight of the forest laws, and two years later, in 1217, they extracted the Forest Charter from the young Henry III. This royal concession disafforested newer areas of forest; redefined more exactly ambiguous forest laws; limited the number of meetings of the forest courts, which were an extra administrative burden thrust on those who lived in the forest; gave archbishops, bishops, earls, and barons the right to take one or two deer (*unam vel duas bestias*) when journeying through the forest, and reduced the punishment for stealing venison from death to heavy fine, or, alternatively, imprisonment followed by banishment.

This charter did not prove to be a final settlement. Its interpretation in the generations which followed led to many disputes, for kings who were short of money were constantly tempted to impose the forest laws more strictly. Edward III and his son, the Black Prince, were under the heavy expense of the French wars in the forties and fifties of the fourteenth century. The Prince, as earl of Chester, administered the forests of Wirral, Delamere, and Macclesfield, and in 1351 he instructed his justiciar to squeeze all the money he could out of the forests. The tenants protested, but the protests were ignored. After two years, public feeling had reached such a pitch that rioting followed a meeting of the forest court at Chester, but it achieved nothing beyond an ineffective demonstration. The dispute was eventually settled by the tenants paying a heavy fine, and the Black Prince blandly assuring them that he was prepared to

The more humble sport of coursing

pardon their past trespasses. A writ issued to William Stanley, chief forester of Wirral, lists 125 fines, amounting to £22 1s. 4d. in all, imposed for offences against the forest law. Both rich and poor were fined, and the correlation between the fines and the offences shows how zealously the law preserved the deer for the arrows of the royal hunters. The abbot of Chester was fined 24s. for cropping four acres of land for three years; Hamon de Mascy 1s. for enclosing a grove; Henry de Hooton 6d. for building a cottage; John de Lasceles 1s. for digging a marlpit, and at least half the offenders one ox or 5s. 4d. for every dog that the wardens had found "unlawed".

Further Reading

H. S. Bennett, *Life on the English Manor, 1150–1400.*

C. S. and C. S. Orwin, *The Open Fields,* second edition, 1954.

W. G. Hoskins, *The Midland Peasant.*

M. W. Beresford and J. K. S. St. Joseph, *Medieval England: an aerial survey.*

III

Street and Market Place

On the eve of the Norman Conquest, before William's soldiers had pillaged and partially destroyed them, Norwich, the third biggest town in England, contained about 1,300 houses, and Chester, the biggest town of the north-west, 500. Domesday Survey credits Exeter, Warwick, and Canterbury with about 250 houses each. Two hundred years later Cambridge was boasting 550 households, Liverpool and Manchester 150 each; and even at the beginning of the fifteenth century there were probably only five towns, London, York, Bristol, Coventry, and Norwich, which had substantially more than 1,000 houses. Figures such as these help to keep the English medieval town in its true perspective. Many towns were little different from large villages. Inside their walls, wooden stockades, earth banks, or whatever means they chose to designate their town's limits, the townspeople had their burgages, the urban equivalent of the peasant's croft, and outside the limits they had their open fields and common meadow lands. Their own harvests supplied the bulk of the food they consumed in the following year, and pigs and poultry wandered as freely in town as in village. Even London was not far removed from the countryside. Fitz Stephen, in his description of the capital in Henry II's reign, speaks of the many citizens who kept hawks and hounds, and hunted regularly in the woodlands and open spaces of Middlesex, Hertfordshire, Kent, and Berkshire. Fields and pastures stood immediately beyond Holborn and the Tower, and each week at Smithfield, Londoners held an agricultural market, in which horses, cattle, pigs, sheep, and farming tools

ST. MARY'S TRAINING COLLEGE
BELFAST.

were offered for sale. The mayor's court did not sit during harvest time, and a law of 1388 confirmed that craftsmen in all towns were still liable to be called into the fields if the harvesters were short of labour.

Chester at the close of the Middle Ages

Most medieval towns had grown out of Anglo-Saxon burhs, or military strong points. They stood on a good harbour, by an important bridge or ford, or at the crossing of two or more main roads. Most were natural communication centres, and this factor, together with the stability and safety ensured first by the Anglo-Saxon garrison and later by the Norman castle, nurtured their infant commerce, attracted craftsmen, and made them obvious sites for courts of justice, royal mints, bishoprics or deaneries, friaries, and schools. Communications in medieval England were notoriously difficult. The Anglo-Saxons had

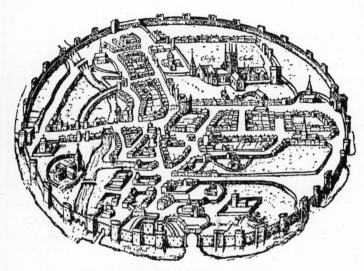

Canterbury at the close of the Middle Ages

Both this and the previous illustration are Elizabethan plans, and show how small important towns remained throughout the Middle Ages

added a network of narrow roads and tracks to the arterial roads built by the Romans, but the only attention all road surfaces received were haphazard and infrequent repairs at the expense of the landowners through whose territory the roads ran. During the drier weather of summer and autumn, pack-horses, with a loaded pannier on each flank, trailed along these dusty ways, but for fully four months of the year thick mud and deep ruts brought most commerce to a standstill. Roads round London were no better than elsewhere: merchants made frequent complaint that in addition to the hazards of footpads and highwaymen, road surfaces were dangerous to life and limb right up to the city's gates. Londoners kept their city's streets in better repair, even if for most of the Middle Ages they restricted paving to short and narrow stretches. Only in the fifteenth century did important towns like Gloucester, Exeter, Canterbury, Southampton, and Bristol begin street paving, and by that time these and other prosperous towns had spread beyond their original limits into slowly-developing suburbs.

The crossing of rivers daunted most travellers. Fords and ferries often involved perilous and wet journeys, and bridges were so few that their crossing frequently made necessary wide and wearisome detours. The crown helped to find the money for the stone London Bridge, which took over thirty years to build at the end of the twelfth century, and many benefactors left money in their will for the repair and maintenance of bridges. But it usually fell to the lord of the manor or to the mayor and aldermen of a town to look after bridges. Some towns con-

London Bridge: an eighteenth-century drawing of the medieval bridge with the houses, mill, and drawbridge which it eventually acquired

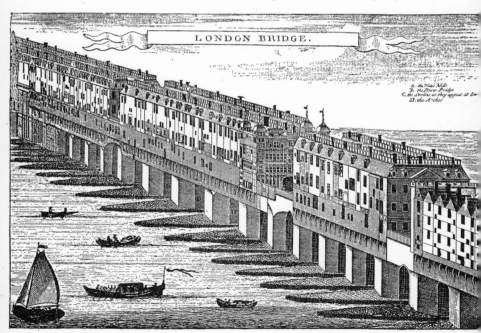

LONDON BRIDGE.

A. the Water Mill
B. the Draw Bridge
C. the Starlins as they appear at Low
D. the Arches

sidered them an expensive luxury, maintained by local rates principally for the convenience of strangers. Townsmen argued that villages round about should contribute to the cost of the town bridge, and when, as was usual, no one volunteered financial help, they were not above letting the wooden structures rot until they be-

The late-medieval bridge at Radcot on the upper Thames

came unsafe, or refusing to replace a bridge when it had been washed away or heavily damaged by flood. Such stupidity acutely inconvenienced townsfolk, neighbouring villagers, and travellers alike, but localism was so strong and economic thinking so narrow, that the impasse could last for years. Occasionally an important local landholder found a way out. In Richard II's reign, Sir Robert Knolles and Sir John de Cobham took the initiative in rebuilding the bridge across the Medway at Rochester, and in 1497, the earl of Derby, spurred on by the prospect of a formal royal visit to Lancashire, built a new bridge across the Mersey at Warrington in place of the one that had collapsed at least a generation earlier. Derby built in stone as, by then, had become the usual practice for important bridges, and to defray the cost of his handsome structure he collected a toll from all users for the next few years.

BOROUGH CHARTERS

Almost all the bigger towns in medieval England, as well as several small towns, such as Warenmouth in Northumberland, Newton in Dorset, and Liverpool in Lancashire, proudly possessed a royal charter, which conferred upon them the title of *borough*, and granted them specified trading privileges and limited rights of self-government. A charter was difficult to obtain before the end of the twelfth century. The inhabitants

49

of most of the hundred or so Anglo-Saxon burhs had acquired privileges of differing worth, but these, which were held personally rather than communally, the Normans chose to ignore. Neither the Conqueror nor Rufus was ready to introduce into England the continental system of granting communal privileges to boroughs. Before 1066 the Cinque Ports, Hastings, Dover, Sandwich, Romney, and Hythe, had jointly undertaken always to have ships ready for the king's use in return for taxation concessions, and before the end of William I's reign Northampton was paying its taxes to the sheriff in one payment of £30 10s. a year, and itself assessing and collecting the individual contributions of the townspeople. But these towns were exceptional, as were London and, after 1066, the communities of French traders, which had established themselves in half-a-dozen towns, including Southampton, Norwich, and Hereford. Not until after 1100 could other bigger towns reasonably hope to be granted trading privileges and a measure of self-government, and not until the reigns of Richard I and John, two kings who were chronically short of money, did smaller towns find it possible, if expensive, to purchase royal charters. By the death of John, "the great borough-charter monger", the crown had issued 330 charters, but two-thirds of them merely confirmed previous grants or redefined land-holding and trading privileges. Thus, in 1155, Henry II issued to the citizens of London a charter, which enumerated certain privileges and confirmed "all other liberties and free customs as well as ever they had them in the time of King Henry, my grandfather". In 1199 the few hundred inhabitants of Lancaster paid John forty marks to seal a new charter exchanging "the liberties of Northampton" for "all the liberties which I have granted to the burgesses of Bristol", which was the key clause in a charter which John, as count of Mortain and lord of Lancaster, had granted the Lancaster burgesses six years previously. To confer on a new borough privileges of an old one helped to create some uniformity among them all, and it reduced to a minimum the exact definition of privileges and rights, which, on some future occasion, the crown might find embarrassing. Not all new boroughs showed the astuteness and caution of Lancaster,

50

which in 1199 sent to the mayor of Northampton for a copy of that town's charter.

Burgesses considered a royal charter worth paying for, even though periodically it had to be renewed at considerable expense, and even though kings tended to look upon boroughs as rich sources of taxation. Details varied, but charters usually freed the burgesses from such servile duties as demesne ploughing and harvesting by allowing them instead to pay an annual fee or fine. Each burgess possessed his own burgage or small-holding. He paid rent for it—one shilling a year, as at Cardiff and Tewkesbury, was a usual, nominal sum—but he could sell it or lease it as he wished. He was free from heriot, and, unlike the peasant, he had no need to seek his lord's consent when he married. Nor did manorial rules usually restrict his freedom to grind corn, bake, and brew. Each burgage carried with it the right to farm strips in the town's open fields, but time which the villager had to spend on his lord's demesne, the burgess could devote to his own business or his croft. He was a freeman, not a bondman. These privileges, together with the protection of the borough court, were open to anyone, freeman or serf, once he had been living in the town for a year and a day, but in most boroughs there seems always to have been a residuum of

The first lines of the Charter which Henry III granted to the burgesses of Liverpool in 1229.

The Charter is written in Latin with many abbreviations. Translated into English the text begins: "Henry, by the grace of God, King of England, Lord of Ireland, Duke of Normandy and Aquitaine, Earl of Anjou, to the archbishops, bishops, abbots, priors, earls, barons, justices, sheriffs, reeves, ministers, and all his bailiffs and faithful people, Greeting: Take note that we have granted, and confirmed by this our charter, that our town of Liverpool (Leverepul) shall be a free borough for ever, and that the burgesses of the same borough shall have a merchants' gild, with a hanse, and other liberties, and free customs . . ."

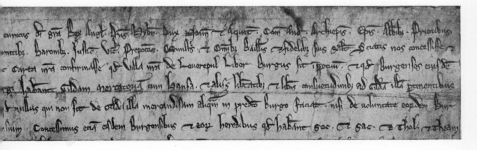

The Common Seal used by the Borough of Liverpool in the Middle Ages

labourers, servants, and new-comers who did not enjoy full burgess rights.

Borough charters protected the trading of the burgesses by restricting the free use of the borough market to them, and by granting the borough court, over which the mayor or his representative presided, the right to settle disputes either between two local traders, or between a visiting merchant, usually referred to as a *foreigner*, and an inhabitant of the borough. The right of *soc and sac* exempted the borough from outside jurisdiction; *theam* gave the court power to compel a receiver of stolen property to disclose how he got it; *infangenthief* conferred the right to try thieves caught within the borough boundaries; and most charters freed the burgesses from such trading charges as *toll, lastage, portage, passage,* and *stallage* in other towns and ports. The charter usually allowed the burgesses to make their own arrangements for collecting taxes, and, through the mayor, to settle their account with the king by paying an agreed sum to the sheriff or, better still, to the exchequer direct. In 1185 the burgesses of Cambridge paid 300 marks for this last privilege. Borough courts inevitably claimed as much jurisdiction as they could extract from the words of the charter, but neighbouring lords of the manor frequently challenged their claims, and the king's justices recognised no boundaries if the king's interests were involved. When the assize judges visited the county town, each borough in the county was required to send a jury of twelve men to represent it. Villages fulfilled the same law by sending the reeve and four others.

In the twelfth and thirteenth centuries many lords of the manor sought royal permission or took it upon themselves to grant seigniorial charters to towns on their estates. Some donors were powerful tenants-in-chief, such as William, earl of Pembroke, who endowed Haverfordwest, or Ranulf III, earl of

Chester, who founded several boroughs, including Macclesfield, Congleton, and Knutsford. Others were princes of the church like the bishop of Winchester, who gave Farnham its charter, and the successive bishops of Durham, who granted Durham, Gateshead, Wearmouth, and Norham the same privileges which Henry I had given to Newcastle. Others again were lesser landholders such as Thomas Grelley, who in 1301 confirmed certain privileges held by "his burgesses of Manchester". If these seigniorial boroughs were good trading centres, they usually prospered, and later, because burgesses preferred the protection of a royal seal to that of a baronial or episcopal seal, they purchased a charter from the crown. But a number of such boroughs, particularly in north-west England, fell victim to fourteenth-century inquiries into the authority for their privileges. Borough rights were formally cancelled, the manor court resumed full jurisdiction, and, as happened to Manchester in 1359, the would-be borough was reduced to the rank of market town.

In most medieval boroughs the gild merchant controlled all trade. Indeed *burgess* and *gildman* were largely interchangeable words. At York, Winchester, and other older towns the gild merchant's authority had spread to town matters in general by the middle of the twelfth century, and in many newer boroughs, burgess status and membership of the gild were virtually identical from the granting of the charter. In his charter to Liverpool, granted in 1229, Henry III followed a usual formula: ". . . that the burgesses shall have a merchants' gild, with a hanse, and other liberties and free customs to the same gild appertaining, and that no one who is not of the same gild shall transact any merchandise in the aforesaid borough, unless by consent of the same burgesses." The gild merchant regulated the borough markets and fairs, and fixed the tolls that should be paid by *foreigners*, though this last power was inevitably restricted by the many royal charters which granted merchants of other boroughs freedom from toll throughout the kingdom.

Gild officials supported borough magistrates in condemning all profiteering and sharp practice, but neither gild regulations nor frequent indictments stopped a minority from giving short weight, using false coins, substituting poor-quality for standard-quality goods, and attempting other forms of dishonesty. Suspicion rested most heavily on bakers, butchers, cooks, and brewers; Langland complained that they poisoned the people "privily and oft". The pillory was the usual punishment for such offences, and, in a way that Gilbert's Mikado would have approved, vendors of bad meat or fish had the offensive flesh burnt under their noses as helplessly they faced the jeering crowd.

Among its members the gild fostered both a strong corporate spirit, and a marked local outlook. Its common seal confirmed corporate intentions and obligations. Gilds were democratic in membership, and most of them, especially the trade gilds in London and some of the wealthier towns, concerned themselves with the welfare and social life of their members. But inevitably as time increased the disparity of wealth among the burgesses, control fell into the hands of the richer merchants. From their number were chosen the civic head, mayor, bailiff, reeve, or provost, and the dozen or two dozen aldermen who formed the council. It is significant that whereas the assize of arms issued in 1181 required all burgesses to arm themselves with tunic, helmet, and lance, the new assize of 1252 differentiated between different categories of burgesses. Those with more than £15 annual worth of land had to possess coat of mail, helmet, sword, and horse. Those with land worth £10, £5, and £2 required arms correspondingly simpler, until those with less than £2 worth of land were instructed to report with scythes, knives, or anything they could lay hands on. These arms, which were regularly inspected, were unlikely ever to be used in serving the king overseas, but towns in the northern counties had to defend themselves against Scottish raiders, ports were always liable to suffer raids by pirates, and every town was obliged by law to keep watch and ward.

A medieval fishmonger

Jealousy occasionally led to armed skirmishes between the burgesses of rival towns, and to intermittent civil war between the ships of two ports engaged in the same trade. For long periods the Cinque Ports carried on feuds with Yarmouth to the north-east, and Portsmouth and Fowey to the west; and "pairs" of ports, such as Poole and Wareham, and Ipswich and Harwich, often allowed their rivalry to become both bitter and violent.

LONDON—"FLOWER OF CITIES ALL!"

In the early years of the twelfth century, London paid half as much tax again as Winchester, more than twice Lincoln's share, three times York's, and twelve times Hereford's. Fifty years later the gap had widened considerably. York had grown markedly more wealthy, but it still paid only a third of London's taxes, which by then had increased to four times Lincoln's new assessment, eight times Winchester's, and almost forty times Hereford's. In 1215 Magna Carta confirmed London's "ancient liberties and free customs both by land and by water", and appointed the mayor of London one of the twenty-five *barons* who were charged to see that the king observed the terms of the charter. For medieval Londoners it would not have dimmed London's lustre by a single candle-power to have realised that their city was only half the size of Paris and little more than one-third that of Venice or Milan, for it was gloriously so much bigger and busier than any other English town. As William Dunbar curiously expressed it at the end of the Middle Ages,

> *London, thou art of townes A per se,*
> *Sovereign of cities, most seemliest by sight, . . .*
> *London, thou art the flower of cities all!*
> *Gemme of all joy, jasper of jocunditie.*

William the Conqueror recognised London's special status when he early confirmed the privileges which it had possessed in Edward the Confessor's day. In a more detailed charter, Henry I freed its citizens from certain royal taxes, the jurisdiction of outside courts, and the necessity of submitting to trial

A rich merchant gives alms to a beggar

by battle, and also, in exchange for an annual payment of £300, gave them the right to collect rents and dues throughout Middlesex and to appoint their own sheriff and justiciar. Stephen later reimposed royal control through a crown-appointed port-reeve and sheriff, and, despite his charter of 1155, Henry II maintained this control and even raised the annual payment, called the farm, from £300 to more than £500. Not until 1190, when Richard was king, did Londoners re-establish their right to elect their own sheriff and pay a farm limited to £300. Even then their success proved temporary, and only heavy payments to Richard and John eventually purchased effective guarantees both that their rights would be respected, and that they should elect their own officers. The borough was divided into twenty-four wards, and the freemen of each ward elected an alderman to sit on the council. Out of the aldermen the freemen annually elected the mayor and two sheriffs, and on each 29th October excited citizens accompanied the new mayor in a colourful procession from the Guildhall, through Cheapside, Fleet Street, and the suburbs of the Strand, to Westminster, where the necessary oaths connected with his office were sworn. London had no gild merchant, but each group of craftsmen and traders, tailors, cutlers, skinners, apothecaries, and the rest, formed a gild of its own. Officials and members of the gild to which the new mayor belonged preceded him in the annual procession: officials of the other gilds dressed in their distinctive liveries, red, gold, white, purple, green, and black, followed. Every gild member was a burgess with full civic rights, and only from the gilds could borough officials be chosen.

Each gild managed everything concerning its particular craft. Under the supervision of its two elected masters, it regulated the recruiting of apprentices, guaranteed the standard of workmanship, dealt with disputes between members, and fixed retail prices. Moreover, each gild tended to colonise a suitable section of the borough. Names like Fish Street, Cornhill, Poultry,

Ironmonger Row, Bread Street, and Cordwainer Street could be interpreted in medieval London as literally as Church Street, Market Street, or School Lane in other towns. The butchers lived mostly round Newgate, the goldsmiths in Cheapside, and the vintners and cooks near the wharves on the north bank of the Thames. Members of the bigger gilds were numerous enough to fill a whole ward, and since wards were responsible by rota for watch and ward and other duties, fellow gildsmen shared civil responsibilities as well as trade and neighbourhood interests.

The poorer members of the gilds and the large number of out-door servants and labourers lived in small houses crowded together in narrow streets. Light and fresh air were badly needed, and the untidy and filthy habits of householders made bad conditions worse. Street cleaning defeated the authorities of every medieval town. Despite regulations often repeated, householders persisted in dumping refuse and sewage in the streets, and allowing their animals and poultry to foul public thoroughfares at will. Few people concerned themselves if dead animals lay about unburied for days, and butchers, who commonly did their slaughtering in the streets, allowed the blood and offal to drain away as best they could. The channel which ran down the middle of most streets became an open sewer, and on hot and humid days, it must have stunk abominably. London's air was full of other noisome smells. Tanning, skin-dressing, and brick-burning took place in a host of small rooms and wooden sheds crowded into narrow spaces behind houses. Fishmongers, like butchers, had no satisfactory way of preserving their wares or disposing of their refuse, and to walk along Cook's Row was to enjoy a strange olfactory experience. Women householders did most

" Betty the brewster" at work

A procession arriving at the church

of London's brewing. Once the brew was ready and the civic ale-tasters had approved its quality, the brewer stuck her ale-stake, or bush, into the front wall of her house as a sign and invitation to her customers. A gallon of ale cost as little as one penny, and drunkenness was common among men and women of all social classes. Langland in *Piers Ploughman* relates how Glutton easily fell to the inducements of Betty the brewster, went into her house, and joined the mixed and drunken company of Tom the tinker, a gamekeeper and his wife, Parson Piers, a ratter, Rose the retailer, a hermit, and the Tyburn hangman. By evening Glutton had "gulped down a gallon and a gill". When he stood to go, he staggered to the door "like a blind singer's dog", and stumbled over the threshold flat on his face.

Obviously such housing conditions increased the danger of both contagious disease and disastrous fire. Medieval people accepted periodic outbreaks of plague as inevitable, and looked upon infancy and childhood as a series of health crises which most children failed to surmount. But they were not quite so fatalistic about fire. They saw that timber houses and thatched roofs were particularly risky, and in 1189, with the memory of

two comparatively recent, devastating fires in mind, the London
sheriff ordered that stone walls, three feet thick and sixteen
feet high, must be built between adjoining wooden houses,
and that stone or tile must be used for roofing. These sensible
rules could only lessen the danger of fire very gradually. It was
bound to be acute so long as houses remained so crowded
together, and brewing, baking, and forge work continued to be
carried out in wooden sheds. No better way of fire fighting
existed than by carrying buckets of water from a well or from
the tubs of water which many householders kept outside their
door. In the thirteenth century, London succeeded in piping
water from springs at Tyburn to a fountain in West Cheap,
but there was neither pressure nor abundant quantity of water.
The authorities intended the fountain to provide drinking water
for the poor, and household water for the neighbourhood. They
expressly forbade brewers, cooks, and fishmongers to use the
water for their trades. Before the end of the fifteenth century,
London had several other conduits and favoured householders
were paying rates for having piped water brought to their
homes, but the chief sources of water still remained the wells,
streams like the Walbrook and the Fleet, and the River Thames
—the ultimate destination of most of London's garbage and
sewage.

Occasionally a splash of rich colour temporarily dispersed the
gloom of the narrow streets. It might
be the dress of a nobleman or rich
merchant as, with his lady and his servants, he pushed his way on foot or
horseback through the crowds of by-
standers; or it might be the scarlet and
blue cloaks of civic dignitaries, or the
many-coloured robes in a procession
of priests. Better still it might be the
brilliance of a royal retinue. Londoners
lavished much ingenuity and childlike
enthusiasm upon the bigger and rarer
processions, and thoroughly enjoyed
annual events such as the mayor's

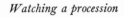

Watching a procession

59

Dancer and dancing dog entertaining the onlookers

formal visit to Westminster, the religious feast of Corpus Christi, and the maypole dancing on May Day. The different gilds presented mystery and miracle plays, in which they enacted allegorical and Biblical scenes either on built-up stages at street corners or on carts which were drawn from point to point in the town. But royal occasions, particularly coronations, demanded the best that could be devised.

When Margaret of Anjou came to London in May 1445 for her coronation, the city surpassed itself. The mayor, aldermen, and gild officials, all appropriately clad in their colourful robes, led her in procession through the streets. Margaret herself, "her hair combed down about her shoulders, with a crown of gold, rich pearls, and precious stones", rode in a litter drawn by two horses decked in white damask powdered with gold, and the people showed their welcome, in the words of one contemporary chronicler, with "divers pageants . . . in royal wise and costly". A second witness spoke of "many devices and stories, with angels and other heavenly things, with song and melody in divers places; and the conduits ran wine, both white and red, for all people that would drink". But coronations happen only rarely, and, despite the prominence given to them by chroniclers and historians, such pageantry and excitement cannot be considered characteristic of medieval London. For months on end those who sought excitement would have to be content with wagering on cock fights or wrestling bouts, or watching a tilting match, or bull and bear baiting.

The wealthier citizens and those noblemen who maintained a town house did not live in any one quarter of London, and their large gardens constituted breathing spaces up and down the crowded town. During the first half of the Middle Ages merchants were not rich enough to build on a baronial scale, but they aped the aristocracy as sedulously as they could. Their hall took up the full height of their house from floor to rafters, and in the two-storeyed back portion of the house, they used the ground-floor room as a store, and the upper floor, which had to be reached by outside stone or wooden stairs, as the solar or private room in which members of the family slept. Kitchen, brewhouse, and dairy were banished into separate outhouses as a precaution against fire. But during the fourteenth and fifteenth centuries greater wealth and better building techniques enabled London merchants to improve their houses considerably. They enlarged the solar, added a number of smaller rooms, and so gave greater comfort and privacy to family living. They increasingly used lead for roofing, tiles for flooring, and glass, instead of horn, linen curtains or shutters, for window spaces. They built stone fireplaces and flues into the walls, and ventilating louvres into the kitchen roof. They began to take a pride in their array of chimneys. Money made in selling wool or trading in wine they spent upon rugs brought to England by Italian merchants, upon tapestries from Paris and Arras and later from London and Norwich, and upon expensive, brightly-coloured wall-hangings of silk, velvet, wool, and brocade. Even wooden panelling had been installed in a few houses before the end of the fifteenth century. Langland, William Harrison the Elizabethan writer, and other traditionalists complained that such "Persian delicacy crept in among us" was a sign of decadence. But most householders appreciated the added comfort

The Smiths' Company enacting the trial of Christ in the streets of Coventry in the late fifteenth century

Stable and house combined

of an indoor staircase, and of a kitchen conveniently placed next to the hall and near the family dining room; and every fifteenth-century lady coveted a fashionable oriel window, in the secluded semi-circle of which she could gossip with her friends or practise on her virginals or viol.

In one of his many valuable studies, C. L. Kingsford describes a house built near the Customs Wharf in the London of Richard II. It had three storeys, the first twelve feet high, the second ten, and the third seven, with a seven-foot cellar under the whole house. The hall measured forty by twenty-four feet, and adjoining it were a parlour or solar, a kitchen, and a buttery. A century later the same house looked very different. The main entrance from Thomas Street led into a wide court yard. Immediately on the right stood the kitchen block comprising a coalhouse, a buttery for wine and ale, a pantry for bread, a larder for salted meats, fish and vegetables, a large kitchen, and three or four store rooms. The hall, which was approached by a short flight of steps from the entrance court, remained unaltered, but behind it the original parlour had been replaced by two bedrooms, a privy, a chapel, a business room, a small intimate parlour, and a *great parlour* in the west wall of which an oriel window caught most of the afternoon and evening sunshine. Over the principal living rooms were garrets used either for storage or servants' beds, and across the courtyard had been built a warehouse and a poultry run.

Surprisingly little thought was given to furniture in the Middle Ages. By the fourteenth and fifteenth centuries the master of a rich household had probably acquired an elaborate bed, fitted with a rope-mesh base to carry the feather-filled mattress, and with canopy and curtains to keep out the draughts. But truckle beds and chaff beds, much less pretentious, were far more commonly found, and other furniture was restricted to tables, stools, benches, cupboards, and large chests, which satisfied the double need of storage and seating. There was probably only one chair in the house, and that would be claimed

Kitchen and dining room of a rich household in the fifteenth century

by the head of the household to lend him distinction when he presided over a formal dinner in the hall. The cheapness of rushes for floor-covering still counterbalanced their obvious disadvantages, and lighting was still expensive and inadequate. Greater wealth made possible a bigger number of candles, which could be carried in a metal lantern, or stuck upon pricket spikes either fastened to the wall or nailed on a large wooden hoop, which rope and pulley could hoist more than head high. Cooking definitely benefited from coal fires burning in the new stone hearths. Kitchen boys turned crank handles to keep heavily-loaded spits revolving before the fire. Cooks used less clumsy cauldrons, pots, and pans made in bronze and earthenware, and had the advantage of more flesh-hooks, grid-irons, and ladles about the kitchen. On the table were plates and cups of English pewter, spoons made of horn and, very occasionally, silver, and dishes of green-glazed pottery. But no forks were to be seen, and if a knife was required at table, men still took their hunting knife out of their belt.

TRADE AT HOME AND OVERSEAS

The speed of the commercial development of any particular area of England in the Middle Ages can be roughly measured by the increase in the number of market towns. Chartered boroughs usually held markets twice a week and fairs twice a year, and lapsed seigniorial boroughs often retained their market rights. In addition lords of the manor periodically gave permission to towns that had no charter to hold a market or fair. Markets, comparatively local affairs, satisfied the weekly requirements of the townspeople and of the villagers who lived up to a dozen miles away, but fairs, much bigger occasions, attracted traders from distant towns and even from abroad. No one in the town could be indifferent to the fair. Religious services and processions marked the opening, and miracle and mystery plays entertained the crowds. Even though the burgesses anticipated big business and the extra stalls spilled over from the usual market place into the adjoining streets, most people were as intent upon merry-making as upon buying and selling. Thriving markets and fairs ensured prosperity to the townspeople, and any threat to that prosperity had to be resisted vigorously. Town authorities did not hesitate to invoke the law and occasionally use force to try and prevent the setting up of new rival markets in their district.

East-coast ports, such as Newcastle, York, Hull, Boston, Lincoln, and King's Lynn, as well as London and such southern ports as Sandwich, Winchelsea, Southampton, Fowey and Bristol, handled a growing volume of foreign trade throughout the Middle Ages, but, because trading patterns altered from time to time, and because there occurred such topographical changes as the silting up of the Lincolnshire Witham and the taking of a new course by the Sussex Rother in the thirteenth century, some ports declined and some increased in prosperity. During the Norman period trade continued to flourish between the Scandinavian countries and the east-coast ports. Ships still sailed from Lincolnshire and Yorkshire as they had done before the Conquest, with cargoes of corn, cheese, and salted beef, and returned with fish, furs, ship-building materials, timber for houses, and hawks which were highly prized by English falconers. During the twelfth century Rhineland traders, especially from Cologne, came in large numbers to London and the south-eastern and eastern towns to sell their good-quality cloth, taffeta, satin, linen, armour, and valuable, highly skilled metal work in gold and silver. In return they wanted to buy English wool. On their heels came the wine importers from western and south-western France, but in the late thirteenth and fourteenth centuries the Italian merchants with their stocks of Mediterranean fruits, silks, sweet wines, and spices from lands east of Suez, were the most powerful group of foreign traders in London. The majority of Londoners heartily disliked the foreigners. They thought they grew rich at the expense of Englishmen, and they blamed them for every misfortune and temporary decline of prosperity. Occasionally their feelings and prejudices burst out in anti-foreigner riots. But by the fifteenth century, although rioting still occurred, sufficient influential Londoners were convinced of the value of close contacts and friendly relations with Burgundian merchants for their commercial interests to become a strong factor in the king's foreign policy. The mutual advantages of trade between south-eastern England and the flourishing textile communes of Bruges, Ypres, Ghent, and Brussels, all within the wide dominions of the duke of Burgundy, made Louis XI as unpopular with London merchants as he was at the court of Philip the Good and Charles the Bold. In 1468 the marriage of Margaret of York to Charles of Burgundy delighted the merchants, because, after a period of uncertainty when Edward IV had appeared to be flirting with a French alliance, it seemed to guarantee a prosperous future. John Paston was one of the gentlemen who accompanied Margaret to Bruges. What he had heard of the wealth and splendour of the Flemish towns and the Burgundian court filled him with the liveliest anticipation. He was not disappointed. He wrote enthusiastically of his visit. "Many pageants were played in her way in Bruges to her welcoming, the best that ever I see. . . . And for the Duke's court, as of lords, ladies and gentlewomen, knights, squires and gentlemen, I heard never of none like to it, save King Arthur's court".

Further Reading

A. Ballard, *British Borough Charters*, Vol. I.

J. Tait, *British Borough Charters*, Vol. II.

C. Stephenson, *Borough and Town*.

J. H. Mundy and P. Riesenberg, *The Medieval Town*.

C. L. Kingsford, *A London Merchant's House and its Owners, 1360–1614. Archaeologia*, Vol. 74.

Boat building in the early Middle Ages

IV

Monastery and Friary

From the second half of the twelfth century, England's trade began to owe more and more to the Church, particularly to the monasteries. During the next hundred years increasing proportions of the wool shipped across the Channel to the spinners and weavers of the Netherlands were sheared from the backs of monastic sheep, and each year in the local markets and fairs monasteries offered for sale bigger quantities of wool, metals, agricultural surpluses, and a variety of manufactured goods. Only generous gifts of land given to the monasteries by generations of laymen made this commercial activity possible. The donors were not all pious men. They were moved partly by a simple, practical faith, which accepted that men could pave their way to paradise by strengthening the church militant with money, land, and goods, and partly by a social fashion, which held that it was the mark of a gentleman to found or enrich a church, or to endow a new monastery or friary. The medieval Church could not help but grow rich, for it had the energy and skill to make good economic use of the thousands of acres of arable and grazing land which it owned. By the time Henry VII ascended the throne, it possessed, according to the testimony of the Commons, about one third of the total wealth of England.

The Normans were enthusiastic churchmen. Their new wealth from the Conquest and the disgust and distaste with which they viewed the small, wooden Saxon churches spurred them on to rebuild parish churches in stone, encourage the enlargement and repair of established monasteries, and persuade the large, Norman monasteries to found priories, or daughter houses, in

England. At Glastonbury, the richest of the English monasteries at the time of the Conquest, abbot Henry de Blois, nephew of king Henry I, built new cloisters, chapter house, gateway, infirmary, and abbot's lodgings. Bishop Gundulf completely reformed the monastery of St. Andrew at Rochester in the days of Rufus, and at nearby Malling began to build a nunnery. The Conqueror himself subscribed towards the cost of building the abbey church at Bury St. Edmunds, and the continental houses of La Charité-sur-Loire and St. Martin at Sées answered appeals from Norman barons, and sent some of their monks to found priories at Northampton and Lancaster respectively. Norman benefactors endowed new monastic houses at Battle, Colchester, Tewkesbury, and Durham, and rescued from decay and neglect many others, including Ely, Gloucester, and the twin foundations of Wearmouth and Jarrow.

MONASTIC ORDERS

This Norman enthusiasm, like that of such contemporary Englishmen as Wulfstan, bishop of Worcester, and Aethelwig, abbot of Evesham, was for Benedictine houses. In Normandy itself, at Jumièges, Bec, Préaux, Fécamp, and other centres, energetic communities of Benedictine, or black, monks radiated the light of reform and religious enthusiasm, which first began to shine in the monastery at Cluny in Burgundy in the tenth century. The Cluniac revival came from within the Benedictine Order, and, together with the general ecclesiastical reforms of Pope Gregory VII, inspired western Europe during the early Norman period; but, though the Benedictines did not cease to lead the monastic movement in England, they were closely followed by other orders, each of which attracted many devotees. The Augustinian canons and the Cistercian, or white, monks came to England in the twelfth century, and founded new houses in which they sought to exercise, the one, their strict interpretation of the rule of St. Augustine of Hippo, and, the other, their ascetic version of the rule of St. Benedict. All canons were priests—an ideal not attained by the Benedictines and Cistercians until the early fourteenth century—and they built most of their houses in the eastern and south-eastern counties, the richer part of England. By contrast, the Cistercians, together with the members of the order of Savigny which they absorbed, sought sites chiefly in deserted parts of the west and north, for the constitution of their order, *Carta Caritatis*, stressed the virtues of simple living and manual labour. No one, they said, could lead the life of a true disciple of Christ if he did not live a balanced life, working

A manuscript illumination depicting St. Benedict adored by the monks of many generations

with his hands as well as his brain, and carrying out the meanest tasks as willingly and as regularly as skilled ones. Consequently, Cistercian communities sought to develop the virgin areas they adopted. From centres such as Fountains and Rievaulx in Yorkshire, Whalley and Furness in Lancashire, Vale Royal in Cheshire, Tintern in the Wye valley, Valle Crucis in North Wales, and Holmcultram in Cumberland, monks and lay brothers cleared the scrub and much of the forest, drained the marshes, ploughed the valleys, turned the wolds and the fells into rich sheep pastures, and, where it was possible, mined iron ore and smelted it with charcoal. The pioneer generations lived hard lives, fully occupied in producing their own food and clothing and selling their excess of goods in order to pay for the maintenance and expansion of their buildings. The devotion of the monks to their ideals so won the admiration of laymen that they showered benefactions upon Cistercian houses. In order to farm the scattered monastic estates, it soon became necessary for the communities to build granges and cells, so that detachments of lay brothers and monks respectively could live near their work. As early as the middle of Henry II's reign the

140 monks at Rievaulx required the help of more than 500 lay brothers and servants to manage their wide lands, and most Cistercian communities soon found that to organise their growing volume of work efficiently, they had to adopt the Benedictine system of monastic officials or obedientiaries, which their founders and predecessors had despised as unworthy of their calling. Later generations had to compromise and relax their rule in other ways if they were to continue to work their

The cellarium or store-house of Fountains Abbey, Yorkshire

estates, but the wealth they created was turned not only into the magnificent churches which they built for the greater glory of God, but also into purchasing power for English merchants in overseas markets.

From time to time in the Middle Ages a new call would ring out for a return to stricter interpretations of the Benedictine or Augustinian rules. In the twelfth century, at the height of the enthusiasm for the Cistercians, the Premonstratensian order of regular canons came to England. It achieved only moderate success, as did the order of Sempringham, a purely English order, founded by Gilbert of Sempringham in 1131. Both these orders, like their predecessors, slipped away from their original

Tintern Abbey, a Cistercian house in Monmouthshire: the transepts of the church

ideals within a few generations, and the only order which kept worldliness successfully at bay throughout the Middle Ages was the Carthusian. In nine English charterhouses, sited in such diverse places as London, Hull, Coventry, and Witham in

71

ST. MARY'S TRAINING COLLEGE
BELFAST.

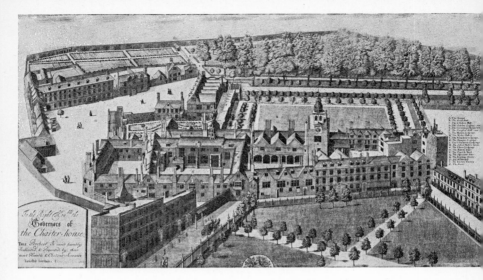

The London Charterhouse in the eighteenth century. The buildings were then used as a hospital, almshouses, and a school

Somerset, the members of this order resolutely followed their ascetic rule, which demanded that each monk should spend most of his time alone in his cell and tiny garden, meeting his brother monks only on Sundays and feast days in order to worship together in the church, and eat a common meal in the refectory.

The Carthusian way of life, too severe for most men, never had any attraction for women, but the Benedictines, Cistercians, and the two orders of canons each built nunneries in which necessarily modified versions of their rule were lived. The Gilbertines, in eleven of their twenty-six monasteries, revived an Anglo-Saxon practice of building double houses. In these the canons, who served the whole community as priests, used the same church as the nuns. But this was the limit of their co-operation. Each set of self-contained, conventual buildings stood apart within the one boundary wall. Even the two daily routines were different, because the canons followed the rule of St. Augustine, the nuns that of St. Benedict. In 1414 Henry V founded at Syon, near Isleworth, the only house of Bridgettines in England. This community of women followed its own version of St. Augustine's rule, and had so strong a devotion to the Bridgettine order that, alone among the hundreds of nunneries in England, it managed to survive the general dissolution in the

72

sixteenth century by moving as a working community to the safety of the Continent. Yet most medieval nuns, like Chaucer's prioress, were more remarkable for their deportment and table manners than for their scholarship or the fervour of their religious faith. They usually came from gentle families; indeed, many would never have been nuns at all had their families succeeded in finding them a suitable husband, or had their husband lived longer. To many gentlewomen to enter a nunnery in middle or later life was almost like returning home, for when they were girls their families had put them in charge of the nuns to be taught to read and write, and to be instructed in good manners and desirable social accomplishments.

THE DAILY ROUND

With the exception of the Carthusians, each order built its houses on the same basic pattern. The cruciform church, vast enough to accommodate the community several times over, towered above the rest of the buildings, a symbol of the community's purpose and an expression of its praise and love of God. Nothing was too rich or magnificent for the Church. Successive abbots and priors lavished money, often beyond the limit of their purses, upon rebuilding unworthy fabric, or adding to internal decoration and treasures. The cloisters tucked themselves into the sunny corner formed by the high, protecting walls of the nave and the south transept. They were the centre of communal life, and the passage way to most other buildings—chapter house, monks' day-room, and parlour on the east; frater or refectory and kitchens on the south; and store house, the cellarer's domain, on the west. The monks' dormitory or dorter was built above the day-room, and was connected by an upper passage and flight of stone steps, the night stairs, to the south transept. The Cistercians, more pressed for room than the Benedictines, housed their lay brothers above the cellarer's stores, and turned their frater at right angles to the cloisters in order to find more kitchen and store room on the south side. Extra buildings, such as the infirmary and the abbot's lodging, had no prearranged position. They were built wherever it best suited the topography of the site and the all important stream, which, in the right order, had to supply water for drinking, cooking, washing, laundering, and carrying away the sewage.

The Rule and customs of the order, enforced by a relentless bell, regulated every minute of every day and disciplined both

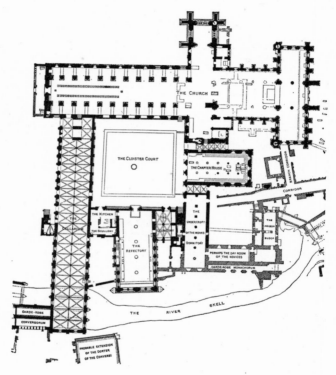

Ground plan of the main buildings at Fountains Abbey, Yorkshire

thought and action. At daybreak, or a little later in the summer, the "careful brother", whom the abbot, according to the Rule, had selected to see that all things were done at appointed times, clanged his bell to rouse the brethren and bid them dress and file into the church for Prime, which was the first daylight service of the seven offices, or services of praise, which the Rule ordained should be sung to honour the precedent set by the psalmist, "Seven times a day do I praise thee because of thy righteous judgments". After Prime the monks went in order of seniority to wash their hands and face at the stone trough in the cloisters. Except in Lent and on other fast days, they then entered the frater for a light breakfast, which was eaten standing in a silence broken only by the boom of the bell already tolling the whole community to Mass. Once Mass had been celebrated the bell directed the monks into the chapter house for the daily assembly, at which the abbot or prior led the community

The stone trough for washing in the cloisters at Gloucester Cathedral

in prayer and praise for the saints and martyrs of the day, punished breaches of discipline, prayed for the souls of benefactors and previous members of the community, occasionally graduated novices into the order, and sought approval for any public business he felt that it was right for the house to transact. From the chapter meeting the monks returned to the cloisters to busy themselves with various activities until the middle of the morning when the bell would ring for Terce followed by High Mass. Those who were priests used this interval to say their private Masses; the novice-master gathered together his pupils for instruction, and others took up their quill pens and manuscripts or attended to the business affairs belonging to their particular office. The celebration of High Mass was the most elaborate and solemn service of the day. On Sundays and major feasts, the officiating priests were fully robed with stole, alb, and chasuble, and the solemn service began and ended with stately colourful processions and deep-voiced Gregorian plain-song.

Dinner in the frater followed High Mass. Even here order and

'The careful brother' rousing the community

discipline persisted. Bells regulated the move from church to the washing trough, the procession into the frater, the timing of grace, and the beginning of the meal. During the serving of the two courses the duty monk read a chosen passage of scripture or scriptural commentary from the refectory pulpit. The bell for Nones, the fifth office, brought to an end the short rest period which followed dinner, and after this brief service came the chief work period of the day, usually an unbroken spell of five hours spent in the gardens, fields, workshops, kitchen, storehouse, schoolroom, office, or study. The vesper bell reassembled the community for Evensong, after which everyone walked through the cloisters to wash their hands, and eat their supper, a one-course meal, in the frater. The day ended with reading in the chapter house, the service of Compline in the church, and the procession of monks climbing the steps to the dorter. But at midnight the sleepless bell knelled them back to duty, and, led by the thin gleam of lighted taper, they made their shivering way down the night stairs into the dark transept to sing Matins and Lauds. Only when they had poured out their praise of God in the exultant words of the last three psalms, and the Lord's Prayer had followed the final exhortation "let everything that hath breath praise the Lord", did the monks reclimb the stairs and return to the austere comfort of their pallet and rough blanket. At daybreak the bell for Prime roused the community from sleep, and the forbidding routine began again.

Several scholars have made gallant attempts to time the activities of the monastic day more exactly, but they have been defeated by the vagueness of the evidence, the obvious effect which the four seasons had upon conditions and routine, and the variations of practice from order to order and age to age. Some communities arranged for a single, unbroken period of rest by retiring about six o'clock in the evening and postponing their Matins until about two o'clock in the morning. They filled the interval between Lauds and Prime with study and devotional reading, not an easy task in the winter when those hours would be particularly cold and dark. In summer the rest period after dinner was usually extended to compensate for the earlier rising. The Cluniacs added extra services to the day, and lengthened to at least six hours the four and a half hours which St. Benedict's rule considered appropriate for daily prayer and praise. But as the twelfth century gave way to the thirteenth, the general effect of change was to reduce the rigour of the routine in many ways. From the beginning it had been necessary in sizable communities to allocate to chosen monks responsibility for certain duties. A precentor was appointed to take charge of the singing, a sacrist to care for the church fabric and ornaments, a kitchener to prepare the meals, an infirmarian to tend the old and the sick, a cellarer to manage the stores and the catering, and a master of the novices to in-struct those who wished to become full members of the order. Such officers were the obedientiaries, each with his own share of the monastic income to spend upon his particular department. But as monasteries steadily added to their estates, matters of business often required such obedientiaries as the cellarer and the bursar to look after affairs miles away from the parent house, and new outside activities compelled abbots and priors to create new offices such as those of

A breach of discipline?

77

wooler, farrier, and forester. In the large communities most obedientiaries needed one or two assistants, and, although it was common for lay brothers and secular employees to help to administer monastic estates, a third or even half the brethren in a thirteenth- or fourteenth-century house could easily be busily occupied with departmental duties.

Christ Church Priory at Canterbury was one of the richest of English monastic houses. In Kent alone it held twenty-one manors, and it had many others scattered over the southern counties and in distant Ireland. It maintained cells of monks at Dover, Oxford, and Monks Risborough in Buckinghamshire,

Submitting to the abbot

and the prior appointed bailiffs to manage most of the manors on the spot. Even so the necessary organisation and periodic inspections could not help but take up much of the time of many members of the community. Dozens of demesne farmhouses and buildings had to be maintained; scores of servants, from bailiffs to swineherds and dairymaids, had to be paid and cared for; and the products of hundreds of cattle, thousands of acres of arable land, and tens of thousands of sheep and pigs had to be efficiently and profitably marketed. The priory's annual profit lay between £2,000 and £3,000, a vast sum by thirteenth-century standards, and yet its monks, big community though it was, numbered on average no more than sixty. There were several other monastic estates just as big. Bury St. Edmunds owned 170 manors, Fountains the whole or parts of 150. Glastonbury enjoyed an income as big as Canterbury's, and in a good year even a 'frontier' abbey such as Furness could earn something approaching £1,000 a year from its unpromising estates on the fells.

Despite many efforts by authorities like the Cluniac and Benedictine chapters-general to prune the monk's day of additional or excessively long services, it became increasingly impossible for monks to attend the daily services regularly, and in their scanty spare time efficiently to manage the business of their administrative office. Nor could many of the secular duties be carried out by men who were obliged to live regularly within monastery walls. For weeks at a time the abbot, with a suitable retinue, had to be away from his community, for he was chief administrator and inspector of his monastery's estates and, like any other baron, was required by the king to fulfil judicial, court, and parliamentary duties. During the summer months when travel was easier, he found himself at his altar celebrating High Mass as rarely as a modern foreign secretary finds himself answering questions in the Commons. Like those of his subordinates, business executives in cowl and robe, who came into daily contact with merchants, bailiffs, and lay workmen, the abbot was bound to lose his single-minded devotion to contemplation and prayer. Whatever he did or wished to do, he could not keep the world away from his monks; getting and spending they laid waste a good percentage of their spiritual lives. In this way necessity forced the first relaxations of the monastic routine

The refectory pulpit at St. Werburgh's Abbey, Chester

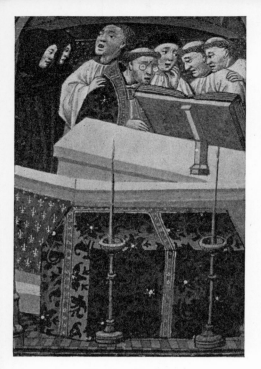

Singing the office

and Rule. Further relaxations came more easily because the less rigid routine encouraged a general desire for still less stringent living. Extra pittances, or meals, regularly included in the daily round, eased the way to habitual meat-eating; frequent business journeys to distant estates or instructions to celebrate Mass in one of the parish churches for which the monastery took responsibility made it much easier to suspend the rule, which required monks not to go outside the walls, "for this is by no means expedient for their souls". Monks began to go on pilgrimage or to leave the cloisters just to enjoy a holiday or pay a social call. The merchant in *The Shipman's Tale* had a young monk as a frequent visitor to his home—

> *as famulier was he*
> *As it possible is any freend to be.*

And none of the pilgrims expostulated when the shipman went on to tell of the merchant's wife arranging to borrow a hundred francs from a man vowed to poverty. The monk who rode among the Canterbury pilgrims expressly rejected the idea that a monk who was "cloisterlees" should be "lykned til a fish that is waterlees", and he readily abandoned to St. Augustine himself the studies and the labours that the Augustinian Rule advocated. If this "lord ful fat and in good point" with his horses and greyhounds was not a typical fourteenth-century monk, he was real enough to be convincing. John Gower, who was writing at the same time as Chaucer, declared in one of his poems that a monk who held an outside office made a poor cloisterer, because he required horse and saddle to journey to and fro and he became accustomed to spending with a generous hand. Changed conditions attracted a different type of man into the monasteries. The ascetics of earlier days were replaced by easier, more natural men, who fully appreciated the good living, comparative security, and administrative and business responsibility offered by the new monastic life.

One of the earliest casualties in this war on austerity was the practice based on the statement of St. Benedict that "they are truly monks when they live by the work of their hands, as did our fathers and the apostles". From the end of the twelfth century most monks abandoned work in the fields, and communities employed lay servants to do more of such necessary tasks as lighting fires, brewing beer, and looking after the elderly and infirm brethren. These changes had the advantage of giving the monks time and opportunity, unhappily frequently rejected, to become more efficient in their administrative tasks, and, where skill and inclination allowed, to spend more time reading, copying, and illuminating manuscripts. Popular belief has considerably exaggerated the monks' reputation for scholarship. The earlier, more austere generations were remarkable for their piety and religious fervour, but not for their learning. From the early thirteenth century, however, certain communities began to take a pride in their libraries, and scholarly members copied and preserved texts written by the fathers of the Church, by poets, philosophers, and historians of ancient Greece and Rome, by canon lawyers, and by medical practitioners. Facilities for study were steadily improved: glazed and screened carrels, or alcoves, in the cloisters made possible more intense and longer concentration by the scholar-

At work in the carrel

81

The type of organ common in churches in the later Middle Ages

monks. From these carrels have come many beautiful, illustrated manuscripts, as well as such commentaries and chronicles, precious to the historian, as were written by Jocelin of Bury St. Edmunds, William of Malmesbury, and Matthew Paris of St. Albans. Some communities were fortunate to have among their members one or more inspiring scholars, who could rouse intelligent enthusiasm for theology and philosophy and direct the study of others, and the founding of colleges at Oxford and Cambridge in the thirteenth century offered abbots and priors a new means of encouraging suitable young monks to devote their life to scholarship as well as to worship and prayer.

THE FRIARS

The vision of the endless worship of God, undistracted by earthly cares and responsibilities, fired the founders of all the monastic orders. They bade their followers withdraw from the world, leave pastoral work and evangelism to the secular clergy, and discipline themselves into privileged, devout families, each under the paternal care of abbot or prior. To St. Francis in Italy and to St. Dominic working in Spain and southern France, this seemed to be a totally mistaken ideal, ignoring Christ's specific command to the Twelve that they should go out into the world and preach repentance and the forgiveness of sins. Therefore, within three years of one another at the beginning of the thirteenth century, these two devoted Christians gathered round them groups of young men, enthusiastic to preach the Gospel to all men everywhere, and literally to obey Christ's instructions to "take nothing for their journey, save a staff only; no scrip, no bread, no money in their purse: but be shod with sandals; and not put on two coats". St. Francis believed that absolute poverty was a necessary attribute of anyone who gave his life to Christ. He even set aside the permitted privilege of wearing sandals, and required his followers, the Grey Friars or Friars Minor, to accept this ideal and to offer themselves as humble men, owning nothing, and ever ready to preach and minister. St. Dominic expected his Black Friars, or Preaching Friars, to lead similar lives, but he also asked that they should be well read in the scriptures and the writings of the early Fathers, for he wanted them efficiently armed to hunt and kill the heresies that he feared were threatening the life of the Church. From the first, learning was a Dominican ideal, as important, if not more important, than worship. St. Francis himself feared that learning was capable of drawing away his followers from their true mission of imitating Christ, but by the second generation of friars the Franciscans in England had become as renowned as the Dominicans for their learning.

England welcomed the friars with open arms. The first group of Dominicans landed in the south in 1221; the Franciscans followed three years later. Both brotherhoods won immediate admiration at court, among the bishops, and in towns and villages. They preferred to have their local head-quarters in the towns, because they were anxious to preach to as many people as possible. A broken-down house, a dank cellar, or a wooden shed gave them all they asked. Indeed, they rejected more weather-proof and wholesome accommodation. Just as they insisted on wearing patched and threadbare habits and walking barefoot even in winter, so they clung to their squalid quarters. They often had gifts enough to build a large, stone friary, but they felt it more in keeping with their vows to knock together a mean house in timber, wattle, and mud, with too little room for the number of friars who were to live there. They never neglected their daily services if they could help it, but they were quite content to assemble in the parish church. When they felt impelled to have their own church, they built it as poverty-stricken as their quarters. Only in their schools were these early friars prepared to tolerate average living conditions. Far from the friary enclosing its members and keeping them from the world, it served the mendicants' purpose best if they were rarely in it, using it merely for occasional rest, refreshment, and services. Their rules forbade them to own anything privately or corporately, and therefore the first generation of friars often gave their friaries into the legal possession of borough authorities.

In the reign of Henry III the friars stood out in startling contrast to the monks. Everyone could see they took their vows more seriously than the monks did. Instead of withdrawing into their cloisters, they shared the trials of poverty with the meanest beggars, and were always ready to earn their food by working in the fields and workshops. They did not demand rents and tithes; at most they begged a few scraps of food when they had not been able to earn any, and some cast-off clothing when their rags would no longer hold together. Little wonder that the coming of the friars inspired a religious revival, that crowds flocked to hear them preach, and that many worthy men wished to forsake all and join them. A steady flow of recruits and gifts ensured rapid development. Forty years after they had first come to England, Dominicans and Franciscans had each established about fifty friaries, most of which housed between thirty and fifty friars. Already the Carmelites, the Austin friars, and a few members of two or three less popular orders had followed the Black and Grey Friars to this country, so that by the end of the thirteenth century there were well over 5,000 friars preaching and ministering in England— one to every 800 or 900 inhabitants. Naturally, the monks did not approve of this remarkable growth. They did not like to see the gifts of the pious laity diverted from the monasteries to the

St. Francis of Assisi, the founder of the Franciscan Order of Friars

friaries, or serious young men preferring to join the mendicant rather than the cloistered orders. They feared that the friars might encourage the townspeople, their intimates, to resist monastic privilege and authority, and they resented the ready support which most bishops gave to the friars in their diocese. Tension increased when the bishops of Hereford and Carlisle, the abbots of Osney in Oxford and Walden in Essex, and a fair number of parish priests resigned their offices and livings to become friars. At Bury St. Edmunds, Coventry, Scarborough, and other places, the established Benedictines and Cistercians strongly opposed the first approach of the friars, and refused them permission to live on their land. But by 1300 there were few if any districts of England not served by one or other of the mendicant orders. Their very meekness and apparent helplessness gave them strength and authority.

The parish clergy too were soon looking upon the friars with suspicion. They knew that they, the seculars, half-educated, slipshod in their duties, and poor not by profession but in spite of every effort to improve their lot, cut poor figures against these trained, often well-educated preachers, who were winning the hearts of their parishioners. The bishops hoped that the friars would inspire the parish priests by their example, but the clergy saw them not as model Christians but as rivals, stealing their congregations from under their noses, damaging their prestige, and, in the second half of the century, accepting fees and gifts for burials, and payments for confession, which normally would have come to them. Thanks to the tact shown by the first generations of friars, and to the restricted burial space in the early friaries, this rivalry between the secular clergy and the friars matured slowly. Later, when the friars, flushed by their success and popularity, became so worldly that Franciscans and Dominicans could quarrel bitterly about precedence and material possessions, the dispute between friars and seculars became more serious and universal than the quarrel between friars and monks. In 1301 the Pope intervened and dictated a compromise. The bull *Super Cathedram* forbade friars to preach unasked in parish churches, limited the number of licensed confessors that each order could have, and ruled that a parish priest was entitled to one quarter of the fees and gifts whenever a friar buried one of his parishioners.

It was from the middle of the thirteenth century, when recruiting was good and the organisation of the orders was becoming more complicated, that the friars began to let their standards slip. As with the monks, necessity dictated the first departures from the rules laid down by their founders. The original friary churches could not accommodate the large congregations which the friars attracted. But once big churches were built more space was available for burials, and consequently more fees and gifts enriched the brotherhood. Scholars could not

A Dominican friar

work indefinitely without manuscripts, writing materials, and suitable rooms, and it was beyond human endurance to maintain for very long the utter destitution and fanatical poverty of the first friars. Warmer clothing, adequate food, and cleaner and more roomy living conditions were common-sense necessities, but at their heels came the employment of servants in the friary, the desire for extravagant living, and, above all, a complete reliance upon begging as the main source of income. Once relaxations began it was difficult to stem the flow. Earning food by labour, and refusing any charity beyond imme-

A Franciscan friar

86

diate necessity became things of the past. Instead, each friary appointed from among its members several limitors, professional beggars, who divided the neighbourhood between them and dragged their sectors systematically for alms. Many communities allowed their limitors to pay an agreed sum into the common purse in exchange for the exclusive right to beg in a specified district, and to put into their own pockets all the money and goods which the laity gave them. No wonder the limitors acquired diabolical skill in raising funds, and an undesirable reputation as unscrupulous oppressors of the poor.

> Beware aye with the limitour
> And with his fellow too;
> If they have mastery in thy bower,
> It shall thee undo,

warned a contemporary of Chaucer, and Chaucer's well-known description of Hubert the friar is full of cutting references to the discreditable practices of the fourteenth century. It is hard to think that within 150 years, many of the successors and self-styled disciples of the saintly Gilbert of Fresnay and Agnellus of Pisa, leaders of the first Dominicans and Franciscans in England, could have degenerated into greedy, specious beggars, well-dressed, scornful of the poor and wretched, and so anxious for money that they were ready to sell absolution for a sufficient sum.

> Ful swetely herde he confessioun,
> And plesaunt was his absolucioun;
> He was an esy man to yeve penaunce
> Ther as he wiste to han a good pitaunce;
> For unto a povre ordre for to yive
> Is signe that a man is well y-shrive.

Friars like Hubert obscured the devotion and good work of hundreds of their colleagues, in much the same way as today the publicity given to divorce figures distracts attention from the large number of happy, lasting marriages. In the fourteenth and fifteenth centuries friars no longer had the advantage of novelty. Their contemporaries took them for granted as a natural item in the medieval scene, but many friars continued to do valuable Christian work in the homes of rich and poor alike, in towns and villages, but especially in schools and the growing universities at Oxford and Cambridge.

Further Reading

David Knowles, *The Monastic Order in England, 943–1216.*
—— *The Religious Orders in England,* 3 vols.
—— and R. N. Hadcock, *Medieval Religious Houses.*
—— and J. K. S. St. Joseph, *Monastic Sites from the Air.*
J. R. H. Moorman, *Church Life in England in the Thirteenth Century.*
Eileen Power, *Medieval English Nunneries.*

A friar preaching to a fashionable congregation

V

School and University

The Church monopolised education throughout the Middle Ages. Almost all teachers and most men whose academic education went beyond the first simple stages were either deacons or priests: indeed, the words *clerk* and *cleric* had the double meaning of one who could read and write, and one in holy orders, and in the fourteenth and fifteenth centuries English law allowed any accused man, who could read two or three verses from the *Psalms*, to claim the benefit of the clergy and be tried in an ecclesiastical court. Theology stood supreme above all other studies, the highest peak of medieval education. The well-trodden path to the summit lay up the steep slopes of Latin grammar and seven years' university study. These brought the student to the shelter of the master's degree at the foot of the final climb. But, from the twelfth century onwards, a gradually increasing number of young men who reached this temporary halting place went off to climb the lower peaks of canon law, civil law, and medicine instead of following the leaders up the sides of theology. A few unorthodox, enterprising souls even began pioneering a new route towards further studies in mathematics and astronomy.

The parents most interested in sending their sons to school and allowing those who wished to go on to the university were the manor-holders in the countryside and the merchants and professional men in the towns. The aristocracy had its own time-honoured ways of educating its children. It sent the girls, who were likely to marry landowners or rich merchants, to a convent, or arranged for them to be taught reading, writing, and simple accounting by a private tutor. The boys, whose destined career lay in soldiering and the supervision of estates, it packed off at the age of seven to be pages in a neighbouring household. For the next seven years these boys spent part of their time learning from the family chaplain or from a grammar master specially appointed for the work. Their academic education rarely went beyond reading and writing, but their household duties helped them to imbibe the manners and customs of their class. About the age of fourteen they graduated to the rank of squire, and, in the company of older men, learned by emulation the more serious and important business of riding, shooting, hawking, and fighting. At the other end of the social scale, the sons of artisans and labourers required the patronage of a local priest or some other stroke of good fortune if they were to be sent to school.

The secular or non-monastic clergy took chief responsibility for education. The fourth Lateran council, summoned by Innocent III in 1215, confirmed that it was part of a bishop's duty to appoint one of his senior canons to be chancellor, or *magister scholarum*, master of the schools, and that the chancellor should teach in the cathedral school and license all other schools in the diocese. This had been the practice both before and after the Norman Conquest, but the twelfth-century enthusiasm for monasteries tended to shift the control of schools from the bishop to the abbot or prior of the local monastery. The peculiar English custom of combining cathedrals and monasteries confused still further this division of authority. At Canterbury, Durham, and eight other diocesan centres, the canons of the cathedral chapter lived a monastic life, and were either Benedictine monks or, at Carlisle only, Augustinian canons; contrarily, the abbots and priors of other monasteries often employed secular clergy to teach those of their pupils who were not postulants for admission to the monastic order. Several old schools, such as those at Huntingdon, Gloucester, and Reading, passed from the control of secular clergy into monastic hands during the twelfth century, and in remoter areas of England, monasteries occasionally provided a teacher for the sons of their richer tenants. But the higher ecclesiastical authorities did not approve of monastic schools. On the other hand they encouraged collegiate churches to open schools for local boys. Early established at Derby, Pontefract, Shrewsbury, and elsewhere, and later to become popular and widespread, collegiate churches were the headquarters of secular canons, who lived a communal life, but whose principal work was to teach and preach to the laity.

SCHOOLS

Until the nineteenth century the Church paid little attention to primary education, and left parents to make what provision they could for teaching children their letters, and guiding them in the first stages of reading and writing. In the Middle Ages most children learned this necessary groundwork from irregular and casual instruction given by busy parents, elder brothers and sisters, or a friendly priest. The only schools which taught at so elementary a stage were the song schools. Their chief purpose was to train choir boys to sing and chant, but since of necessity they had to teach their future choristers to read as well as sing, they were often asked to take young children, girls as well as boys, whose parents had no intention of putting them into the cathedral or church choir. In her story to the Canterbury pilgrims, the Prioress describes such a school, and tells how Christian children

> *. . . lerned in that scole yeer by yere*
> *Swich maner doctrine as men used there,*
> *That is to seyn, to singen and to rede,*
> *As smale children doon in hir childhede.*

Before they left the song school the most intelligent or regularly-attending pupils were capable of pronouncing and writing single words, reciting the Lord's Prayer and Creed, and chanting canticles and psalms. They could mouth Latin words and understand the purport of the main prayers and

A school at work

Another school at work

canticles, but usually they could not construe the simplest sentence. To acquire a knowledge of Latin, the next necessary stage in their education, the boys had to move to a school which taught grammar.

Medieval Latin was a living language, in which educated people from all over Europe regularly conversed, scholars wrote and taught, priests conducted services, and merchants and lawyers transacted their business. Just as modern English uses phrases and idioms which Shakespeare never knew, so medieval Latin used words and constructions unknown to Cicero. At best, it was a homogeneous language still virile though past its greatest vitality; at worst, it was merely a Latinised form of Norman French or English, with no constructions of its own and using numerous borrowed words lightly disguised with a Latin suffix. The students' first stage in its conquest was to master the basic grammar. The teacher dictated section after section of Donatus's *Ars Minor* or Priscian's *Grammar*, and the boys learned each section by heart. A good memory served the medieval schoolboy well, for he had no reference or text books. He could gradually build up a collection of notes, but hand-written books were too scarce for general possession, and dictionaries did not exist. From basic grammar he graduated through easy texts like Aesop's *Fables* to selected passages from Virgil, Ovid, Horace, the *Vulgate*, and the writings of the early Fathers of the Church. But ability to read Latin was not enough. It was necessary to write Latin prose and verse, and to converse and discuss in the language. To encourage this side of the work, many schoolmasters forbade their senior pupils to speak anything but Latin on school premises. Boys of twelve, thirteen, and fourteen years managed to do this with varying degrees of accuracy, and once they began to study rhetoric and logic as well as grammar, they were regularly called upon to make speeches and to debate in Latin. The pride of a medieval schoolmaster was a pupil, fourteen years old at most, who could dispute in Latin nice points of grammar and logic before admiring parents and friends.

Grammar, rhetoric, and logic constituted the *trivium*, the first major stage in medieval education. In Norman times, instruction in these subjects was offered by the cathedral schools, the few collegiate churches of those days, and other schools licensed by the bishops, but none of them necessarily restricted themselves to the *trivium*. If they had capable teachers and ambitious pupils, they would teach one or more of the advanced subjects of the *quadrivium*—arithmetic, music, geometry, and astronomy. A few, especially the cathedral schools, had usually an advanced pupil or two studying theology or canon law. Some twelfth-century schools achieved reputations which attracted advanced students from all over England and even from across the Channel, and they soon tended to leave to lesser schools the teaching of basic grammar, logic, and rhetoric, and to close their own doors to pupils who were not already proficient Latin scholars. This specialisation eventually produced, on the one hand, the universities to offer the advanced teaching, and, on the other, the grammar schools to feed the universities with suitable students and to teach

The title-page of a Latin primer, printed in England in 1516, but copied from a fifteenth-century original

The oldest class-room at Eton College

those boys who did not wish to do more than learn Latin. Some grammar schools remained under the direct control of a cathedral chancellor, the head of a monastery, or the warden of a collegiate church. Others were endowed by trade gilds or financed by chantry bequests, and, in the fourteenth and fifteenth centuries, a large number were founded by merchants and landowners, who wished to provide grammar education in the town or village in which they were particularly interested. By the end of the Middle Ages there could have been few towns and large villages without a grammar school. London had at least five; Bristol, Norwich, and York two or three. On average throughout the country each school served 6,000 or 7,000 people. But medieval grammar schools were very small. Most of them were housed in a single room or part of a church, and pupils rarely numbered more than twenty-five or thirty. In many grammar schools they could be counted on the fingers of one hand. Schools such as William of Wykeham founded for seventy scholars in fourteenth-century Winchester, or as Henry VI founded at Eton in 1440 for four clerks, six choristers, and twenty-five schoolboys, must not be taken as typical medieval schools. One master only was appointed to most grammar schools, and he had to teach all pupils, at whatever midway stage they were between an elementary knowledge of reading and an ability to speak and write Latin. He would count himself fortunate if he had an usher or pupil-teacher, who could relieve him of some of the elementary teaching and share the maintenance of discipline.

The medieval schoolboy had no reason to like school, and many reasons for hating it. Day after day he learned nothing but Latin, except a little rhetoric and logic if he stayed at school long enough to qualify for such lessons. The master's method of teaching never varied, and the boy was required to sit or

94

stand in the classroom for eight
or nine hours a day, learning by
heart, and often without understanding, grammar rules or Latin
passages dictated to him. Games
were usually forbidden, holidays
largely restricted to Church feast
days, and severe corporal punishment automatically inflicted for
both misbehaviour and single

Wrestling and a round of quarter staff

mistakes in repetition or translation. Educational practice
scarcely changed during the two centuries that followed the
Middle Ages, so that Shakespeare's audiences readily appreciated Jaques's whining schoolboy "creeping like snail un-
willingly to school", and Romeo's assertion that

> *Love goes toward love, as schoolboys from their books;*
> *But love from love, toward school with heavy looks.*

Nor did medieval schoolboys find any sympathy at home. It
was a universally held maxim that sparing the rod spoiled the
child, and parents were as ready as schoolmasters to "trewly
belassch hym tyl he wyll amend", as Agnes Paston advised her
son's teacher to do, adding significantly, "and so ded the last
maystr and the best that ever he had att Caumbrege". Another
fifteenth-century mother advised her daughter not to curse her
children if they rebelled and would

> *not bow them low,*
> *But take a smart rod and beat them in a row,*
> *Till they cry mercy and their guilt well know.*

In *Piers Ploughman's Vision*, Reason charged the merchants to
chasten their children, and not
pamper them with soft living
conditions, and the thirteenth-
century rules at Westminster
School were full of instructions
concerning prompt and severe
chastisement.

The perennial game of whip and top

Playing at tournaments

Such hard and sustained suppression naturally built up a pressure which periodically exploded into violence and hooliganism. Some schools acknowledged certain days for letting off steam. William fitz Stephen, describing twelfth-century London, told of schoolboys arranging cock fights on Shrove Tuesday, tournaments in Lent, a water carnival at Easter, archery in the summer, and skating and bull baiting in the winter. Later in the Middle Ages school authorities usually permitted and even encouraged boys to practise archery, but they set their face against football, which inevitably developed into an unorganised rough-and-tumble dangerous to life and limb. Several cathedral schools indulged in traditional tomfoolery on St. Nicholas's Day, 6 December, and the Feast of the Innocents after Christmas. On 6 December the boys elected one of their leaders as bishop, and he in turn appointed his dean and canons from among his school friends. Together on the Feast of the Innocents, commonly known as Childermas, these temporary dignitaries conducted a topsy-turvy service, and were afterwards entertained in state by the senior clergy. The ceremony originated from a desire to mark the feast with a practical demonstration of putting down the mighty and exalting the humble and meek, but it degenerated into an unholy, sacrilegious romp and a parody of church services. Despite periodic condemnation by ecclesiastical authorities, the practice persisted in several schools throughout the Middle Ages. Even the saintly Henry VI made provision for it in the statutes of Eton, and Colet, reformer though he was, ordered the boys of St. Paul's School to attend church on Childermas Day in order to hear the boy-bishop's sermon.

CHANTRIES

One of the characteristics of church life in the later Middle Ages was the endowing of chantries

Games with hoops

to ensure regular masses and prayers for the souls of the founder and his family. Chantries developed from a tradition that dated from the Conquest, by which laymen were invited to contribute towards an extension or rebuilding of a monastery or parish church, in exchange for regular prayers offered for their welfare both here and hereafter. The names of these *confratres* or *familiares* were entered on a bead-roll, or occasionally in a splendidly-bound book such as the *Liber Vitae* at Durham or the *Catalogus Benefactorum* at St. Albans, so that out of ignorance future generations of priests should not fail to say the promised regular prayers. A relatively poor man could afford to be a *confrater*, but it took a rich man or a corporation, such as a religious or trade gild, to find sufficient money to endow a perpetual chantry. Not only did it require the building and furnishing of the chantry chapel, but also it called for a gift of land, which could yield an annual rent big enough to pay the stipend of the chantry priest. In certain dioceses, including London, York, and Lincoln, chantry endowments became increasingly popular in the fourteenth and fifteenth centuries, and many a priest, in Chaucer's words,

> . . . *ran to London, un-to seynt Poules,*
> *To seken him a chaunterie for soules.*

The terms of the endowment nearly always required the chantry priest to do auxiliary duties, and the most common requirement was teaching. Many chantry schools offered free or cheap education, usually at the grammar school stage, and by the time the Reformation began to disturb the medieval religious world, about 2,000 such schools were open in England and Wales. Some were dissolved with the monasteries with which they happened to be associated; the remainder perished a few years later, after the passing of the Act for the Dissolution of the Chantries at the beginning of Edward VI's reign.

UNIVERSITIES

Despite the poor communications of Norman and Angevin England, news of an exceptional teacher expounding theology or law could set serious students in distant places bundling their few possessions together and setting out on foot or scraggy horse to sit at his feet. One successful teacher attracted others, and in this way certain towns established reputations as centres of learning. In the twelfth century London, Lincoln, and Exeter

Prince Arthur's Chantry, Worcester Cathedral. The burial place of Arthur, son of Henry VII

had well-known schools in canon law and theology, and in the thirteenth century teachers in Salisbury and Northampton drew to their classes many students in both these subjects and in civil law. But the schools which took deepest root were at Oxford. There, during the reigns of Henry I and Henry II, Theobaldus Stampensis, a scholar from Caen, Robert Pullen, a renowned theologian who was later created a cardinal, Geoffrey of Monmouth, the Welsh historian, and Robert of Cricklade, prior of St. Frideswide's in Oxford, built so lasting a reputation for this conveniently situated centre that new generations of students and teachers continued to go there almost automatically. In 1209,

A university class

the hanging of two students by the townspeople, in revenge for the murder of a woman, nearly closed Oxford's schools permanently, for, half in fear and half in protest, students and teachers hurriedly left to seek safer conditions in Reading, Stamford, and Cambridge. Five years later, after King John had made his peace with the pope, the papal legate led the students back to Oxford, sternly rebuked the townspeople for their previous conduct, and placed the schools under the jurisdiction of the bishop of Lincoln, or of the chancellor whom he cared to nominate as his deputy. From this point in its history, if not from 1201 when Master J. Grim was described as *magister scolarum Oxonie*, master of the Oxford schools, Oxford can safely claim that its various schools constituted a *studium generale*, or university. Within the next ten years the friars began to arrive, and there followed half a century of wise leadership and enthusiastic teaching and studying, in which two names, Grosseteste and Bacon, stand out above the rest. Robert Grosseteste served as tutor to the first generation of Franciscan friars in Oxford, and then, in turn, was elected chancellor of the university and bishop of Lincoln. Roger Bacon, a pupil of Grosseteste, was one of the most distinguished of medieval philosophers and scientists.

Cambridge University cannot claim so spectacular a beginning. There is no agreed date for its foundation, but certainly the migration of some Oxford scholars to Cambridge in 1209 contributed to its reputation as an educational centre. Henry III encouraged groups of displaced, foreign scholars to make new homes there, and in a royal writ of 1231 recognised the status and authority of the chancellor. But not until the fourteenth century did Cambridge free itself from the active interference of the bishop of Ely, and only in the following century did it begin to attract students in numbers comparable with those at Oxford. Lack of medieval registers and college accounts at both universities makes speculative all assessments of attendance figures, but it would appear that Cambridge never had more than a few hundred students before the fifteenth century, whereas within its first hundred years of existence Oxford's student population approached 3,000, and then dropped to about 1,000 in the fifteenth century, when political conditions were more unstable, when the effects of the Black Death were still apparent, and after some leading teachers had alienated more orthodox minds by flirting with the views of John Wycliffe.

Medieval universities were very different from modern ones. Term and vacation did not divide the year as precisely as they do today. Students came and went as they pleased. Most undergraduates did not stay long enough to take a first degree, and those that did stay qualified by four years' residence, and by a series of disputations or oral examinations with senior members of the faculty. Written examinations, though not unknown, had nothing of their present-day stature or significance. For many years university authorities accepted no responsibility for feeding or sheltering either students or teachers. The chancellor and his proctors took reasonable measures to maintain discipline and prevent town and gown from coming to blows, and in 1231 Henry III instructed the mayors of Oxford and Cambridge and the sheriffs of the two counties to suppress disorder, weed out those rogues who posed as students, and compel landlords to exact fair rents from their student-lodgers. The problem of excessive rents was partly solved by groups of students each electing a graduate principal and clubbing together their slender resources to lease a house for a limited period. Alternatively enterprising graduates rented

Another university class

*Merton College, Oxford: Mob Quad, the oldest part of the College, and the
mid-fifteenth-century tower*

houses, and, as principals, let rooms to undergraduates. The chancellor held the principals responsible for the good behaviour of their students both in the town and in their *hall* or *hostel*, as Oxford and Cambridge respectively termed these houses. No hall had many members—a number between ten and twenty was usual—and, since each hall was held on a short tenancy, they were all liable to lapse into private residences. H. E. Salter has described Hincksey Hall, Oxford, at the beginning of the fifteenth century. It contained the medieval equivalents of ten study-bedrooms at annual rents ranging from £1 to 5s. The principal administered the accommodation and did some teaching, but the catering was in the hands of a manciple, who, like Chaucer's manciple at the Inner Temple, was probably widely suspected of watching his profits too assiduously. Different halls attracted different types of students. Newcomers from Wales, Ireland, or the North sought rooms in halls where fellow countrymen were already installed, and, as ever, more advanced students preferred not to live with freshmen. But it was not until the fifteenth century, when the number of students was declining, that the halls at Oxford had sufficient accommodation for the authorities to insist that undergraduates should live in halls and not lodgings.

Most university students were much younger in the Middle Ages than they are today. To matriculate at twelve years old was exceptional, but at fourteen quite common, and since many boys stayed at Oxford or Cambridge one or two years only, the average age of undergraduates was no higher than that of middle-school pupils in present-day grammar and public schools. From the moment they arrived in the university town and began to walk the narrow crowded streets among townspeople, students, and tonsured clerics sporting green, blue, or scarlet gowns, these boys found themselves forced back on their own resources. They had to seek their own lodgings, and decide for themselves what lectures to attend. No one in authority was concerned how they spent their time, providing that they did not run foul of the proctors and their armed attendants, or were caught in the streets after the curfew bell had rung at nine o'clock. The more decorous part of the student body consisted of a fair number of parish priests, monks, or friars studying for their first degree, bachelors of arts attempting to qualify for their master's degree in quiet hours snatched from teaching grammar, and masters of arts continuing their studies in medicine, law, or theology. Since it required at least three years' residence to graduate from bachelor to master, and from five to seven further years to qualify in any of the advanced subjects, many medieval scholars spent all their adolescence

Merton College Library: the west wing, built in the fourteenth century. The furniture is, of course, much later in date

and young manhood at the university. For most of those years almost all students were in holy orders, and they spent part of their time teaching or carrying out priestly duties.

The colleges of medieval Oxford and Cambridge were not built for undergraduates, but for small groups of graduates who wished to live a communal life while reading for a higher degree. About 1270, Walter Merton, charitable chancellor of England, built Merton College to be a home for about thirty graduates, who would live and study under the supervision of a warden. Two or three years later, University College was built out of

Jesus College, Cambridge, which the Bishop of Ely founded in 1497 by converting a Benedictine nunnery into a college

funds which William of Durham had left in 1249 to maintain masters of arts studying theology, and before the end of the century Peterhouse had been established at Cambridge on the same pattern as Merton. The number of colleges increased steadily. At Oxford, Balliol College, endowed as part of a penance by Sir John de Balliol, followed on the heels of Merton and University, and the following century saw Exeter, Oriel, Queen's, and New College founded in Oxford, and King's Hall, later absorbed by Trinity College, Michaelhouse, which did not survive, Clare, Pembroke, Gonville, Trinity Hall, and Corpus Christi College founded in Cambridge. The general purpose of all these colleges was the same, but each had its own characteristics. Exeter housed one chaplain and a dozen bachelors from the diocese of Exeter who were studying for their masterships; Oriel ten bachelors or masters most of whom were reading theology; Clare twenty graduates reading arts or theology, with an odd one or two allowed to read law or medicine; and, conversely, Trinity Hall twenty graduates reading canon or civil law, with an odd one or two allowed to read theology. All members of colleges, whether they were in holy orders or not, had to be unmarried. Indeed as soon as a scholar married, the church and the universities closed their doors against him; he had to earn his living as a grammar-school master, a doctor, a lawyer, or out of the professions altogether.

Despite the renewal of the war with France and the political unrest which culminated in the Wars of the Roses, the founding of university colleges did not slow down in the fifteenth century. Lincoln, All Souls, and Magdalen Colleges were built at Oxford, and Cambridge showed evidence of her increasing vitality by founding Godshouse, which developed into Christ's College and set out specially to train grammar-school masters, King's College endowed by Henry VI, Queens' College, the joint memorial of the Lancastrian Margaret of Anjou and the Yorkist Elizabeth Wydeville, as well as St. Catherine's and Jesus Colleges. In the last few years of the fifteenth century, colleges began to admit undergraduates. They handpicked a few from the hundreds available, and often required them to do menial duties in the college in exchange for board and lodging. An undergraduate who agreed to live in college sacrificed his freedom for better conditions. No longer was he able to change his rooms as he wished. The warden or master of the college overlooked his work, and the routine of the community compelled him to live a more ordered life. The college day bore some resemblance to the monastic day. It began about six o'clock, and regular religious services, announced by the chapel bell, divided it into recognised working hours and recreational hours. Lectures and tutorial sessions, each lasting well over the modern allowance of one hour, took up most of the working time. Dinner at ten o'clock in the morning and supper at five in the evening were both eaten communally, and some colleges practised the monastic habit of appointing a junior to read to the members during each meal. For more than half the year it was difficult to work in private rooms in the evening, because they lacked both light and heating. Therefore, the college reserved the last hours of the day for debating, story telling, and singing, when one or two candles and one fire could serve many people. The prospect of moving

Accompanying the singing at a sing-song

ST. MARY'S TRAINING COLLEGE
BELFAST.

from the snug circle in the common room into the cold, dark bedroom above must have been most uninviting when the night was black and there was frost on the ground, but the fall of the log fire and the last splutters of the candles were signals as inescapable as the bell for Compline that another college day had come to its end, and that the time was at hand for the seniors to seek their feather beds and the juniors their straw mattresses.

Further Reading

A. F. Leach, *The Schools of Medieval England*. Also the criticism of Leach's argument by A. G. Little in *English Historical Review*, Vol. xxx, pp. 525–9.

H. Rashdall, *The Universities of Europe in the Middle Ages*, edited by F. M. Powicke and A. B. Emden, Vol. III.

H. E. Salter, *Medieval Oxford*.

G. H. Cook, *Medieval Chantries and Chantry Chapels*.

A. W. Parry, *Education in England in the Middle Ages*.

VI

Scientists and Theologians

During the first hundred years of its existence, Merton College remained unsurpassed in Europe as a centre for scientific and mathematical studies. Many of the early fellows, following the lead of Robert Grosseteste and Roger Bacon in the first half of the thirteenth century, gave their lives to experiment and observation, and helped to transform medieval scientific thinking. Richard of Wallingford, a Benedictine monk and later abbot of St. Albans, and Simon Bredon, who took his medical degree in 1330, were among those Merton men who invented more accurate astronomical instruments for measuring altitudes and fixing the position of planets. About 1320 Wallingford constructed a clock, whose many geared wheels ingeniously engaging together not only ticked away the minutes and hours, but also indicated the state of the tides, the phases of the moon, and the position of the sun and planets in the heavens. He set up this complicated machinery, one of the earliest public clocks in England, at St. Albans Abbey, where no doubt it caused considerable wonder and curiosity, and put out-of-date the mural sundials, which cloud or dull skies invariably reduced to impotence, and which were often marked only for the times of the principal church services. In the early fourteenth century, William Grizaunte and John Ashenden, both fellows of Merton, studied eclipses and the movement of the planets. John Maudith and William Rede, the builder of Merton Library and afterwards bishop of Chichester, led and encouraged the many scholars who patiently compiled astronomical, tide, and mathematical tables in those dimly-lit, sparsely-furnished rooms.

The face of the Medieval Clock in Wells Cathedral. The outer circle marks the hours, the star moving round the inner circle the minutes, and the centre circle the days of the month and the phases of the moon. At the hour four knights charge round the turret above the clock

Much of this early work of calculation and observation was tedious and painstaking, but these Merton scholars set a small band of successors on the road, which, going by way of Jean Buridan and Nicholas Oresme, two later fourteenth-century French scientists, eventually led in the sixteenth and seventeenth centuries to the experiments and conclusions of Galileo.

The pre-eminence of Merton College did not last beyond the middle of the fourteenth century. The zeal of the first generations of scholars for personal experiment and enquiry gave place to a willingness to accept the figures and conclusions of previous investigators, and other colleges, both at Oxford and Cambridge, began to make increasing provision for astronomical and scientific studies. Neither John Somer, a Franciscan, nor Nicholas of Lynn, a Carmelite friar, the two leading Oxford astronomers of the later part of Richard II's reign, were Merton men. In their day, Chaucer sent Louis, his son or his ward, to Oxford, and because of the young man's interest in mathematics and astronomy, gave him a portable astrolabe together with his own description and explanation, in English, of how to use the instrument. He also copied from the "kalendres of the reverent clerkes frere I. Somer and frere N. Lenne" (Lynn) astronomical tables to help "litell Lowys" in his work. When Chaucer came to tell a suitable tale for the Miller, he based it on Oxford and made one of the main characters a student of astronomy, who could forecast the weather "whan that men sholde have droghte or elles shoures".

GREEK AND ARABIC TEXTS

It is possible to look upon this Oxford activity during the reigns of the first three Edwards as following an English tradition of scientific study, which began with Bede and his contemporaries, who were surprisingly observant and enquiring about tides and moon changes. But it would be more realistic to see it as a logical development from the reintroduction into Western Europe during the twelfth century of the scientific writings of Aristotle, Euclid, and Ptolemy. Since the sixth century theology had eclipsed Greek science in Europe. It was generally held by early medieval scholars that the Fathers of the Church for all time had both interpreted the Scriptures and defined man's relationship with God and the universe. Further experiment was superfluous, re-examination presumptuous, and critical thinking dangerously near to heresy, for by the very nature of things nothing could be accepted as true unless it fitted the traditional teaching of the Church. The history, which one generation taught the potential teachers of the next, did not attempt to separate fact, surmise, and legend: in astronomy and natural history, reasonable hypothesis and nonsensical theory won equal approval. The commentaries of Boethius on some of the philosophical writings of Aristotle and Plato were the only Greek-inspired writings available to Englishmen before late-Norman times, for in such Christian works as St. Augustine's *City of God*, or in the practice of the few doctors who based their knowledge on the traditions derived from the Greek physicians, Hippocrates and Galen, the classical influence was so muted and transformed

A gnomon with a compass needle, dated 1451. Under the compass needle there is a line, the function of which was to indicate variation, thus proving that the necessity for this correction had been known before the time of Christopher Columbus

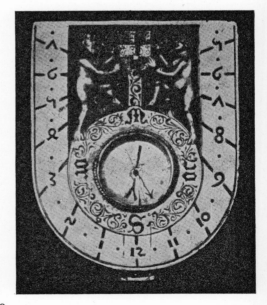

Face of an astrolabe of Chaucer's day

that it could not be isolated or measured. In pre-Norman and Norman England, most learned men clung fast to authority, despised secular knowledge, and concerned themselves exclusively with the salvation of souls. They had no wish to match their individual reasoning against the accumulated wisdom of the Church. They agreed with St. Ambrose that discussions on the nature and position of the earth would not help man in his hope of the life to come, and they accepted St. Augustine's final conclusion on faith, that man should rest content to be ignorant of the mysteries of the heavens and the earth.

Fortunately contemporary Islam took a different view. Arabic theologians succeeded in reconciling Greek philosophy with the teaching of the Koran, and Arabic doctors, alchemists, astronomers, and mathematicians studied their Greek masters and made striking advances of their own. Like Karshish, Browning's fictional Arab physician, they were "not-incurious of God's handiwork", and restlessly investigated such problems as why "pricks and cracks befall the flesh through too much stress and strain", so that the "wily vapour" of the soul manages to "slip back and rejoin its source" before the natural span of life has ended. From the middle decades of the twelfth century, European scholars such as Adelard of Bath, Robert of Chester, and Michael the Scot lived in Spain or Sicily, two of the no-man's lands between Christendom and Islam, and translated into Latin many Arabic manu-

110

scripts. Gradually, they made available to western European scholars both Arabic medical knowledge, Arabic numerals, and the *Arithmetic* and *Algebra* of the Persian mathematician, Al-Khowārizmī, as well as the writings of Aristotle, Archimedes, Euclid, and other Greek philosophers and scientists. Within two or three generations translations of these manuscripts, most from Arabic and a few directly from the Greek text, had been so assiduously copied and distributed to centres of learning that the potential range of European knowledge had widened considerably. Aristotle became a name to conjure with: he, above all other Greek writers, won unquestioned authority among western scholars. His writings did both good and harm. They encouraged a more logical and penetrating method of reasoning, but, where his conclusions were based on faulty premises, as happened frequently in natural history, the stamp of authenticity which Aristotle's name conferred discouraged most scholars from reseeking the truth by their own reasoning and experiment. If they got so far as observing phenomena which contradicted or did not fit into Aristotelian theories, they tended to distrust their own work rather than reject the master's conclusions. To deny the truth of Aristotle's writings was tantamount to heresy in some academic quarters.

Robert Grosseteste was an enthusiast for the new Greek and Arabic learning. Both at Oxford in the twenties and thirties of the thirteenth century and at Lincoln after he had been appointed bishop in 1235, he invited Greeks to come to England to help

Back of the astrolabe

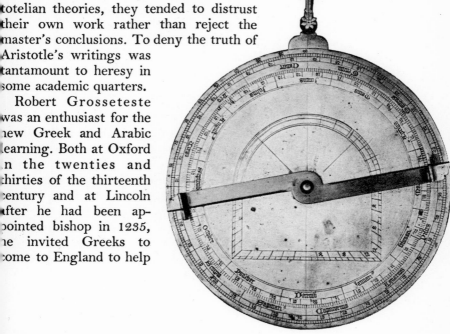

Robert Grosseteste, bishop
of Lincoln

translate manuscripts into Latin. He learned
Greek himself in order to further the work.
But Grosseteste did not allow Aristotle to
sweep him off his feet. In theology he remained a traditionalist, preferring the philosophy of St. Augustine to that of Aristotle:
in secular studies he approved Aristotle's
method of analysing observed facts, but he
was not content to accept Aristotle's conclusions. He urged his pupils, particularly
the Franciscans, to study as many Greek and
Arabic manuscripts as they could, but also to
observe and experiment themselves. Guided by his reading of
Euclid's *Elements* and Aristotle's *Posterior Analytics,* he set an
example by investigating for himself such natural phenomena as
weather, heat, colour, and sound, by trying to make the Christian
calendar conform more exactly to the movements of the sun and
moon, and, above all, by devoting much thought and time to a
mathematical and experimental study of optics. Inspired by the
work of the Arabic mathematician, Alhazen, he came very near
the modern explanation of the rainbow; he used lenses to assist
failing eyesight; he observed the effects of refraction, and even
developed a theory that light travelled in wave-like movements.
For Grosseteste light became the most important element in
the universe. It derived, he believed, straight from God. Acting
on inanimate matter, it had originally created the universe and
all life in it, and the degree of virtue in every human being
depended on the intensity of the light he received from God,
and the way in which he radiated it to others.

Roger Bacon, the Franciscan friar who was born in Somerset
in 1210, became as renowned a scholar as his teacher Grosseteste. He worked for many years in Oxford, where his reputed
study-observatory, with its uninterrupted view of the heavens
to the south, remained a show-piece on Folly Bridge until
eighteenth-century road wideners pulled it down. Bacon, like
his master, stressed the importance of personal experiment and
investigation. He warned his pupils not to allow their own
thinking to become sterile through showing too great a

112

reverence for tradition and authority, and forbade them both to reach conclusions too quickly, and to maintain them in the face of contradictory observations. His forthright teaching brought him into serious trouble both within the Franciscan order and in the church in general. Fortunately, before the general of the Franciscans put him into gaol, the temporary protection of the enlightened Pope Clement IV gave Bacon time to set down his experiments and interpretations in three manuscripts, *Opus Majus*, *Opus Minor*, and *Opus Tertium*. Much of Bacon's work sounds surprisingly modern. His experiments on mirrors and lenses developed Grosseteste's work on optics. He calculated more accurately than hitherto the length of a year, and attempted to estimate the size of the countries in the world. He even dreamed of such fantastic possibilities as mechanically-driven ships and piloted flying machines. But naturally all his speculation was handicapped by typical thirteenth-century interests and beliefs. His studies of optics attempted to explain the mechanism of magic mirrors as well as of human eyes. His careful observation of a comet in 1264 was followed by an exposition of how its appearance affected the troubled politics of that year in England. He was ever hopeful that man might one day find the philosopher's stone, and, like all his contemporaries, he did not doubt that the earth was the centre of the universe.

THE MEDIEVAL UNIVERSE

Not until the middle of the sixteenth century did Copernicus publish *De Revolutionibus Orbium*, the first clear statement that the earth was one of several planets revolving round the sun. Hitherto learned and ignorant alike had accepted the evidence of their eyes that the earth was static, and that sun and moon revolved around it. Most later medieval scientists agreed that the earth was not flat but spherical. They explained eclipses

The study-observatory of Roger Bacon on Folly Bridge, Oxford

and the phases of the moon by the fact that the heavenly bodies revolved on their own axes as they circled round the earth, and they accounted for the apparent difference in the sizes of the sun and the moon when near the horizon or high in the heavens by a theory of refraction. But, although the astronomers puzzled over the odd behaviour of the planets, which seemed to move round the earth at different speeds and sometimes even to slip back in their orbit, they never succeeded in making the mental effort, which would have allowed them to stand outside themselves and see the world and its neighbours in space from a viewpoint other than their own.

Scientists and theologians together constructed an elaborate picture of a universe consisting of nine transparent, hollow spheres, all of different sizes and all encircling the earth. The spheres were *glassy* or *crystalline*; according to Aristotle they had no weight, but they were strong enough to carry along with them their allotted burden of heavenly bodies. On the inner one rode the moon, on the fourth the sun, and on the eighth all the fixed stars. Mercury, Venus, Mars, Jupiter, and Saturn were usually allocated a sphere each, and the outside sphere of all, *primum mobile*, was believed to supply the motive force for the other eight. Different medieval writers varied the details of this universe. Some followed Aristotle, others Ptolemy, whose theories were known chiefly through the text book, *De Sphaera Mundi*, written by John Hollywood of Yorkshire towards the middle of the thirteenth century, and destined to hold the field for three hundred years. But both Aristotelians and Ptolemists agreed that the outside sphere could never be seen by man. It carried no star or planet; it was the crystal sphere which marked the outer limits and divided God from His creation. Quite literally, heaven was "above the clear, blue sky", and hell was below the feet of man in the central hollow of the earth.

For the medieval scientist matter consisted of four elements, earth, water, fire, and air. Each element had an inherent compulsion to be at rest in the place where it belonged. Whenever earth and water gained freedom of movement the *gravity* within them compelled them immediately to get as near to the centre of the earth as possible, but on the other hand the innate *levity*

Schema præmiſſæ diuiſionis.

DE CIRCVLIS SPHÆRÆ.
CAP. III.

B

Plan of the Universe taken from Cosmographia *by Peter Apian of Bavaria, who was a contemporary of Copernicus but a traditionalist in belief*

of fire and air caused them to rise towards their respective allotted spheres, which were for ever revolving round the earth. Ever since Adam and Eve had been thrust out of the Garden of Eden, the four elements had been in constant turmoil, and because all living things contained some measure of each element, it was essential for human life on earth that the elements should remain mixed. To accommodate man on dry land in this temporary life, some earth had been forced from the central mass and compelled to float on top of the water, which in a free, natural state would have covered the earth core of the world. It was widely believed that this area of dry land was restricted to the northern hemisphere. It stretched south to the equator, north to the arctic circle, west to the western coasts of Europe and North Africa, and, until Marco Polo showed otherwise, east to the Ganges. Most significantly, at the centre of this irregularly-shaped mass of earth stood the city of Jerusalem.

Everything above the moon was eternal, everything below subject to decay. Man, however, enjoyed a unique privilege, because mixed with the earth, water, air, and fire of his body was a fifth, unknown, incorruptible element, personally given by God to each of His creatures made in His image. On the death of the human body, this divine spark or soul had the natural desire to rise to God beyond *primum mobile*, but whether

115

it would be accorded such bliss depended upon its conduct on earth. It could be condemned to eternal torment in hell.

What happened in the macrocosm of the heavens medieval man believed was reflected in the microcosm of human life. God ruled His universe through agents. To the fixed stars, predictable in their movements, he delegated the government of such regular aspects of human life as the succession of the seasons, and the cycle of birth, growth, decline, and death: to the changeable planets, he entrusted such unpredictable happenings in human life as sudden death, famine, plague, or the birth of twins. Both the incorruptible stars and the planets were God's creatures, and acted as He willed. Therefore, it followed logically that if astronomers and astrologers could predict and interpret the movement of the planets, they could forewarn men of coming benefits or menacing disasters, and even foretell a child's destiny from the position of the planets at his birth. When obvious mistakes were made and threatened calamities did not occur, men did not question the fundamental reasoning, but put the blame on the astrologer's inability to interpret correctly.

> *For in the sterres, clerer than is glas,*
> *Is writen, god wot, who-so coulde it rede,*
> *The deeth of every man, withouten drede.*

Reducing a dislocated shoulder

Medieval man saw nothing quack in astrology. To him it was a serious study for scientists, and not an art by which charlatans could make money out of a credulous, ignorant public. Ashenden and Rede of Merton College were seriously believed to have foretold the Black Death after studying an eclipse of the moon, and, both individually and jointly, these two scholars wrote several treatises on such topics as, "The consequences of the coming conjunction of Jupiter and Mars on 7 August 1349", and, "The significance of the conjunction of Saturn

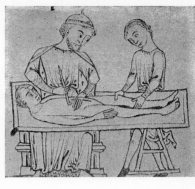

Examining an apprehensive patient

and Jupiter in October 1365 from calculations made at Oxford in March 1357". To forecast movements of planets eight years ahead, both the fourteenth and the twentieth centuries would readily attribute to scientific skill, but the fourteenth century placed a similar or even higher value on the astrologer's ability to interpret the effect of planet movement on human destiny. It did not conflict with their Christian faith to believe that propitious movements of Venus could ensure the success of a marriage, or that a comet's appearance in the heavens heralded strange and unusual happenings on earth.

Just as astronomy and astrology were hard to separate, so were medieval chemistry, alchemy, and medicine. The alchemists sought in vain the formula which would turn base metals into gold, but in their search, by methods no subtler than trial and error, they acquired much useful knowledge about metals. Out of this knowledge came improved methods for smelting iron, better mixtures for bronze, and new alloys suitable for the specialised needs of clockmakers, bell-founders, makers of astrolabes and surgeon's knives, and the manufacturers of cannon and of the machinery used in corn mills and fulling mills. Similarly, the physicians, befogged as they were by their belief in charms, evil spirits and the influence of the planets upon their patients, nevertheless hit upon several sound remedies. Chaucer's Doctour of Phisyk, "a verrey parfit practisour", though "grounded in astronomye" had studied many medical authorities from Hippocrates and Dioscorides to Gilbertus Anglicus and Dr. John of Gaddesden. Dr. John had read medicine at Oxford as recently as the first years of the fourteenth century. He served Edward II as royal physician, and wrote *Rosa Anglica*, which he becomingly claimed excelled all other treatises on the practice of medicine. Even in previous centuries there had been no lack of medical textbooks, but the more successful medieval doctors built up their own fund of practical knowledge from observation and experience. Towards

117

the end of the Middle Ages some doctors risked outraging lay opinion, and began to fortify their knowledge of anatomy by dissecting corpses. Yet none of this more scientific practice and thinking dispelled the fogs of tradition and superstition. The best medical men believed implicitly in the efficacy of complicated prescriptions which contained a dozen loathsome ingredients from powdered diamonds to crushed beetles. They looked upon Saturn and the zodiacal signs of Taurus and Pisces as hostile to success in surgical operations, they recommended hanging a magpie's beak round the neck to cure an inflamed throat, and they believed that a king's personal touch was the only effective remedy for scrofula, the king's evil. Nor did doctors understand the importance of cleanliness in the Middle Ages. Bathing was not a medieval habit, and when a physician ordered a patient to have a bath, he was less interested in cleaning the body of his patient than in observing the effect of the medicinal herbs which he put into the water.

THE THEOLOGIANS' VIEW OF SCIENCE

The new approach to learning initiated by the translations of Greek and Arabic manuscripts could not help but affect theological studies. Aristotle's logic and use of human reason so threatened the sovereignty of faith and so disturbed the conventional disputations of the schoolmen, that Paris, the leading theological centre in western Christendom, rejected Aristotle and all that he stood for, until, in 1225, a new generation of Parisian scholars accepted the newly-available Greek texts as proper subjects for study. By the middle of the century,

Taking out an arrow which must have made a serious wound

Albertus Magnus, a Dominican friar of Cologne, had begun, and his pupil, St. Thomas Aquinas, was to continue, the task of fusing Christian, Greek, and Arabic thought into one amalgam. They argued that though faith, which came to man through divine revelation, was distinct from and superior to reason, the reasoning power of man was God-given and could properly be used to strengthen faith. Those scholars who were not Christians could only construct their philosophies on the restricted base of what they could learn from experiment and human experience, but it should be possible to produce a *Summa Theologiae*, a synthesis of Christian and secular thought, which would be the epitome of all human learning. This Aquinas attempted to do. Where faith so opposed reason that synthesis became impossible, Aquinas

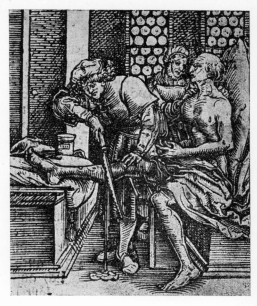

An amputation: the nurse presses on the jugular arteries to numb the pain

gave his support to the Christian interpretation. He accepted the Greek view of the universe as a working hypothesis, but he rejected Aristotle's theory of the eternity of the world in favour of the traditional Christian belief in a definite moment of creation, and he never doubted that man had been created in the image of his Creator. For Aquinas the world had far more importance and reality than it had had for the Fathers of the Church. He reasoned that, since the Christian faith taught that God had created the world and that man's soul was divine, man should seek evidence of God and His methods in God's world. To study terrestrial things could help in the understanding of heavenly things. Science could aid theology, providing it remained content to stay in those fields of knowledge in which reason could work effectively.

Thomism, as the philosophy of St. Thomas Aquinas came to be called, continued to satisfy many theologians even after the Middle Ages had given place to the Renaissance, but it did not lack its medieval critics. Among the most prominent of its opponents in fourteenth-century Europe were two Franciscans, a Scotsman, John Duns Scotus born in Roxburgh, and an Englishman, William of Ockham born in Surrey. Both accepted

Aquinas's distinction between faith and reason, but both went further and strictly confined faith and reason to their own respective philosophical territories. Duns drastically reduced the number of theological truths which could be proved by reason, and Ockham denied that reason could ever demonstrate the truth of any theological belief. Belief rested on faith and authority alone. Neither of these philosophers accepted the implication in Thomism that God worked logically, and that it was possible to find out something of His methods from a study of His creatures, both animate and inanimate, on earth. Instead they held that God did what He wished freely, that He was not limited by physical laws of any kind, and, therefore, that logic and reason were powerless to confirm the existence of God, or to prove anything that lay beyond the physical limits of the world. Yet neither Duns nor Ockham was prepared simply to accept the faith of the Fathers of the Church. Duns agreed with previous theologians that there must be a first Being, and that by His very being He must be omniscient and infinite. But, he went on to argue, since all creation, past, present, and future, was the result of God's will—for God does just as He wills—man could not possibly explain God's methods, or know anything which God did not wish him to know. Ockham went further. He divided all knowledge into "intuitive knowledge", which was derived from direct awareness of specific objects (for example, a mother and her child, or two men fighting), and "abstractive knowledge" which concerned universal concepts (for example, mother love, or human enmity). Abstractive

Left: *Helping a patient to inhale aromatic fumes*
Right: *Instructing a patient how to treat his skin disease*

knowledge could be derived only from intuitive knowledge. It was clearly impossible, said Ockham, for man to have intuitive knowledge of God, and therefore it followed that man could never have abstractive knowledge of Him either. Man would never *know* that God existed, or that the universe was finite, or that it required an external force to set the universe in motion. To Ockham belief in God and in salvation must always be a matter of faith, in which reason had no place.

Treating an infected ear

Philosophical and theological arguments such as these were heard only in the universities and a few ecclesiastical centres. The ordinary priest or laymen held to his simple beliefs. He did not wrestle with the problems of faith and reason, or attempt to distinguish between God's absolute power or God's ordained power. He remained content to live his life, teach "Cristes lore and his apostles twelve", and trust to the infinite mercy of God. But, as so often happens, the rough conclusions, if not the full arguments, of the new philosophies seeped by teaching and discussion from the active minds of the few into the receptive minds of a greater number. In time they influenced articulate public opinion and the outlook of the rising generation of students. Increasing literacy among the middle-class laity speeded this process, so that fourteenth-century English thought is characterised by increasing uncertainty and mounting anti-clerical feeling. Duns Scotus, William of Ockham, and their fellow philosophers were not alone responsible for this, but together with other causes, such as a growing national feeling engendered by the Hundred Years War, the presence of a *French* pope at Avignon during the Babylonian Captivity, and the devastating effects of the Black Death, their influence can be seen both in the Statutes of Provisors and Praemunire, 1351 and 1353, which limited papal rights in England and forbade Englishmen to appeal to Rome against or over the head of English courts, and also in the spread of Lollardism. Wycliffe, the founder of the Lollards, declared that salvation could be earned individually but not "communally" out of the store of grace held by the Church, and maintained that the only justification for clerical authority was the righteousness of individual clerics. Both Ockham and Wycliffe had strong influence in Oxford in the second half of the fourteenth century.

The freeing of reason from faith should have made the scientist's work easier. If God were not bound by natural law, and if man could never know God, then it followed that anything the scientist discovered could not possibly affect man's faith in God. This logic the Church did not easily accept. Ockham, like Roger Bacon before him, suffered imprisonment for his teaching, and though Ockhamism came to be widely accepted among scholars for a time, it did not become part of permanent orthodox belief. As is well known, even as late as the seventeenth century, Galileo was forced under torture to recant new scientific discoveries, because they conflicted with the traditional beliefs of theology.

Further Reading

R. T. Gunther, *Early Science in Oxford.*

H. Butterfield, *The Origins of Modern Science, 1300–1800.*

Robert Grosseteste, ed. by D. A. Callus.

Gordon Leff, *Medieval Thought from St. Augustine to Ockham.*

A. C. Crombie, "Science", Chapter 18 in *Medieval England*, edited by A. L. Poole.

— — *Augustine to Galileo. The History of Science, A.D. 400–1650.*

Preparing medicines

VII
Technologists and Craftsmen

Despite a revival in the study of Thomism and a widespread demand among Sunday newspaper readers for the weekly guidance of their favourite astrologers, twentieth-century England finds little but historical interest in medieval theology and science. On the other hand, it fully appreciates the extant work of the medieval builder, wood-carver, glazier, and illuminator. The theories of medieval cosmologists and alchemists can be dismissed as *fantastic* or *quaint*; but men and women still catch their breath when they first enter King's College Chapel in Cambridge, or for the first time see Lincoln Cathedral dominating its diocese from its hill-top site. They still gaze with wonder at the carved canopied stalls at Chester Cathedral and at the beautiful illumination work which most major libraries periodically display. Thousands go each year to admire such early examples of medieval crafts as the St. Nicholas font at Winchester or the famous tapestry at Bayeux. Even the ruins of medieval skill inspire love and respect. Curiosity takes most visitors to Stonehenge, and sentiment to Shakespeare's house or Nelson's flag-ship; but architectural appreciation is probably dominant in most holiday-makers' minds as they visit Carisbrooke Castle or move through the grounds of Rievaulx Abbey.

The practical needs of warfare and living have long outdated the most efficient of medieval castles and houses, but all except a handful of English cathedrals and major churches are medieval buildings repaired and enlarged by successive generations. The foundations of most village churches date back to pre-Reformation days, and though the long list of rectors or vicars may hang framed at the back of a nave wholly rebuilt out of Victorian prosperity, and though the stained glass in the east window may perpetuate the memory of those parishioners who perished in

The western face of the twelfth-century St. Nicholas font in Winchester Cathedral

two world wars, the overall design of the church would still be familiar to the men who built its first tower or carved its first gargoyle six or eight hundred years ago.

Yet the carefully preserved cathedral and parish church and the ruined splendour of abbey and castle portray too rosy a picture of medieval building. The thousands of mean wooden houses, the hundreds of precarious, plank bridges, and the faulty stonework in scores of the buildings which still stand have all disappeared. Only historical records now tell of the towers that were blown down at Bury St. Edmunds, Chichester, and Evesham, of the central tower that collapsed at Ely, or of the badly-built columns at St. Albans that suddenly broke and brought the roof crashing into the nave. The wide mortar-joints and ill-fitting stone blocks of much early work, as well as such picturesque survivals as Chesterfield's twisted spire

Rievaulx Abbey, Yorkshire: the thirteenth-century Choir and Presbytery, looking east

and the crazy angles of occasional doorways and window spaces, are all salutory reminders that medieval builders learned from their failures. They had no arts or skills now lost to modern tradesmen. By decades of patient uneconomic work, and by the sacrifice of wealth which other ages would have devoted to improving living conditions, the Middle Ages at length transformed rents, tithes, taxes, gifts, and credit into those soaring spires whose "silent fingers" continue to point the way to the medieval heaven.

THE MASONS

To build in stone or brick in medieval times was so expensive that none but the richest could afford to do it. Usually, but by no means always, the king and the great nobles built castles in stone. The church, often compelled to use temporary wooden accommodation for years on end, eventually managed to pay for the piecemeal erection in stone or, less commonly, in brick of most of its churches, monastic houses, and colleges; and in later times, borough councils occasionally called in masons to build an important bridge or a new public building. All other buildings were of timber, at best founded on stone footings and roofed with tile or stone flags. Consequently, every town and sizable village had its own carpenters, tilers, thatchers, plasterers, and daubers, but the masons had to go where their work led them, and, like modern civil engineers, live for a month or a life-time on the job in hand. Their mobility, made easier by the absence of national barriers during most of the Middle Ages, helped technical knowledge and stylistic changes gradually to spread throughout Europe. That Norman fashions of building should have come to England in the years immediately after the Conquest seems natural enough. It is, however, not so readily appreciated why, during the reigns of Rufus and Henry I, masons working on Durham Cathedral should have been using new techniques akin to those being used in contemporary work in the Netherlands and the German states, or why the design of the abbey at Cîteaux in Burgundy should have had a widespread influence on twelfth-century building designs in England, or why the masons who built the famous west front at Wells in the early thirteenth century should have followed a new fashion set by Canterbury and Lincoln, instead of continuing the regional architectural style of the earlier parts of the cathedral.

The crown and the richest abbeys employed permanent masons, but the crown did not hesitate to impress any extra labour required for its own works. When he thought it necessary to increase the rate of castle-building in North Wales, Edward I, like Priam in Lydgate's early fifteenth-century description of the building of Troy,

Thirteenth-century masons and carpenters at work

. . . made seke in
every regioun
For swiche werkemen as
were corious,
Of wyt inventyf, of cast-
yng merveilous; . . .
Or swiche as werne able
for to serve
With lym or stoon, for to
raise a wal.

Edward III and Henry VI
forcibly recruited skilled labour for the more rapid building,
the one of Windsor Castle, the other of Eton College; and since
masons were nearly always fully employed, these royal demands
could not be met without bringing to a standstill less urgent
work. Paying Peter meant robbing Paul.

Because they were so itinerant, the masons could not fit into
the local gild system. Instead they formed lodges on each
building site, and inside the lodge buildings dined, slept, and
organised their workshop. They looked to the lodge to provide
them with tools, and the lodge leaders insisted upon satisfactory
rates of pay, a good standard of workmanship, and the training
of the right number of apprentices. They enjoyed few leisure
hours in daylight. During the winter months, often defined as
from Michaelmas to Lent, they began work at dawn—"als erly
als thai may see skilfully by day lyghte", to quote the words of
Masons' Ordinances at York in 1370—and they finished at
dusk, although when time pressed it was not unknown for them
to work on with the aid of candles and cresset lights. In the
summer months, with two hours allowed for meals and rest,
the working day could spread over fifteen or sixteen hours—
from "the son risyng . . . until itte be namare space than tyme
of a mileway before the sone sette". Sundays and the principal
saints' days were holidays. Local custom determined which
saints' days should be recognised as holidays, and each year
different festivals merged with Sundays, but medieval workmen
could usually look forward to at least twenty-five or thirty

127

"red-letter" days in a year. Christmas, Corpus Christi, and a dozen other major festivals customarily carried with them a half-holiday on the eve. But holidays had their dark side, because as a rule workmen were not paid for any of them, nor for idle hours enforced by frost, snow, and heavy rain.

The Norman kings and barons thought little of their masons. Their heavy, cumbersome fashion of building, using pillars unnecessarily massive and walls unnecessarily thick, called more for organising labour than for exercising building skills. But as the squat Norman tower and sunken, rounded window gave

Masons busy on a royal building

way to the loftier and more delicate architecture of later times, the mason's status and importance increased. It became the custom to appoint a master mason to design and supervise each building, and the employer, whether king, nobleman, abbot, or mayor, confined himself to supplying the money, and discussing and approving proposed plans. From the early thirteenth century it was widely recognised that the master of the king's masons was the unofficial doyen of English masons, and holders of that important office were often called upon to act as consultant engineers, or to supply working drawings and designs for buildings for which they were not directly responsible. Henry Yevele, the king's master mason in the reigns of Edward III and Richard II, helped to plan the rebuilding of Westminster Abbey,

The Nave of Canterbury Cathedral designe
Henry Yevele, Richard II's Master M

supervised the walling of the city of Canterbury, designed the new nave and cloisters of Canterbury Cathedral, advised Lord Cobham on several of his building projects, managed quarries and sold stone, as well as carrying out his official work of keeping the Tower of London and Westminster Palace in good repair. Of course the services of the average master mason were not sought so assiduously, but none could afford to be a narrow specialist for he was responsible for the choice of stone, the soundness of the foundations, the overall plan of the building, the details of windows, pillars, arches, and timber work, and the organisation and well-being of the necessary labour force. After a disastrous fire in 1174 the chapter of Christ Church, Canterbury, appointed William of Sens, a well-respected French builder, to rebuild the ruined choir. Gervase, one of the monks, described him as "a man active and ready and as a craftsman most skilful in both wood and stone". Unfortunately, in the fifth year of building, William fell from the scaffolding of the upper vault, and was so severely injured that, after a short period in which "a certain ingenious and industrious monk" took charge, he resigned his office to another William, "small in body, but in workmanship of many kinds acute and honest".

Early medieval masons seem to have carried their plans and designs more in their head than on parchment, but during the fourteenth and fifteenth centuries working drawings, elevations, and ground plans came into general use. Even so, the master mason required to be constantly at hand if the drawings were to be properly and safely followed. His employers did not always pay him sufficiently for his responsible work. Henry III fully appreciated the worth of John of Gloucester, *magister cementarius regis*, and Edward I paid Walter of Hereford, who took charge of the building of Caernarvon Castle and other royal works, 14s. a week, almost six times the wage he paid to journeymen masons. William de Hoton, who succeeded his father as chief mason at York Minster in 1351, received a guaranteed annual salary of £10 for life, subject to the proviso that when old age or incapacity should prevent him from carrying out his duties, he should surrender half of it to his deputy. But all master masons were not so fortunate as the leading few. Most received slightly higher wages than journeymen, enjoyed greater security, and, if they were lucky, lived on a small pension when their active days were ended.

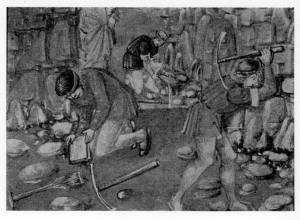

Quarrying stone

STAGES OF CATHEDRAL CONSTRUCTION

The difficulty and cost of transport made it advisable for builders to use local stone. Quarries near Shepton Mallet supplied the stone for Wells Cathedral and Glastonbury Abbey. The early Oxford colleges drew chiefly from Headington and other Oxfordshire quarries, and Lincoln Cathedral from Ancaster, twenty-five miles to the south along Ermine Street. Special requirements or individual fancy sometimes made it necessary to bring stone from a distance. King's College Chapel used Yorkshire stone, and with considerable difficulty ten carts carried from Nottingham to Windsor the alabaster used for the reredos in St. George's Chapel. In the thirteenth century, Norwich Cathedral purchased stone at Caen, and subsequent freight charges more than trebled its initial cost. Builders in many parts of England bought Purbeck marble for statues and columns, when it became fashionable to decorate churches with contrasting stone. They reduced costs a little by using water transport wherever possible, and by cutting and shaping much of the stone at the quarry. Wooden and canvas templates helped the quarry masons to get shapes and sizes right. From the thirteenth century onwards, the more celebrated quarries, such as those at Corfe, York, and Burton, set up workshops to make prefabricated tracery, shafts, images, and tombs in standard patterns, as well as to cut stone to specific designs supplied by the customer. They sent out the most delicate work rough-dressed in order to reduce the risk of

131

damage in transit, but, for the most part, all they left the local mason to do was to fix the prefabricated ornament into position. The increasing use of bricks in the fourteenth and fifteenth centuries partially solved the transport problem, because suitable clay could often be found where building stone was not available. The bricks that Henry VI used for Eton College were burnt at nearby Slough.

Both in the quarry and on the building site, the limitations of their tools slowed down the medieval mason's work. To split stone from the natural seam they hammered in iron wedges, and then levered it away with crowbars or stout pieces of wood. For rough dressing they used axes, and for the final cutting and shaping mallets and chisels. All their cutting tools, though they were shod with steel, easily blunted, and were in constant need of filing, grinding, or reworking by the blacksmiths. Yet most medieval churches reveal with what skill many masons managed these imperfect tools. It is difficult to imagine much more delicate work than some of the stone foliage which still decorates the chapter houses of York and Southwell Minster, or the transepts of Wells Cathedral.

The cautionary example of a number of leaning walls and fallen roofs convinced most master masons that every building required solid foundations. They would instruct their labourers to dig deep to find the solid earth, and then, to make doubly sure, would crush broken stone into it, or drive in wooden piles with a crude pile driver, or cover it with heavy flat stones bonded together by mortar made from lime and sand. The walls rose very slowly from the foundations. Each stone of the double row of faced blocks, ashlar, had to be carefully fashioned. The surface of the inside wall had to be made

Decorative stone foliage at Southwell Minster, Nottinghamshire

smooth, and the space between the two rows packed tight with rubble. Frequently the winter caught the masons with an unfinished wall wide open to the weather, and they were compelled to thatch it or cover the top with grass sods until the dangers of frost had passed. Once the wall had risen more than four or five feet above ground, rope and pulley tackle had to be used to lift the stones into position. Tables set on tall trestles enabled the masons to build to about twenty feet high. After that they required scaffolding. Their labourers constructed a criss-cross of long poles lashed together with withies or bast rope made from the flexible inner bark of the lime tree, and on this framework they fastened hurdle platforms. More precariously they sometimes set up platforms on iron brackets driven into the stone work, but once construction got beyond the reach of the longest ladders, the masons had to work from the unfinished building itself. In the fourteenth and fifteenth centuries the increasing use of hoisting machines saved much time and labour. They were variously designed and called by different names— trace wheel, gin, verne, and crane—but all used the principle of the lever, windlass, or pulley, or a combination of two or all three of them. The smaller machines were worked by hand, the larger occasionally by water-power but more commonly by a "walk-wheel" or treadmill. But even with these later devices, considerable danger and difficulty must have been encountered raising stones to the masons

How the Thirteenth Century imagined the Tower of Babel was built

building the spire of Salisbury Cathedral, or hoisting into position the mighty oak beams, three feet square and over sixty feet long, which formed the frame-work of the wide octagonal central tower of Ely. Fortunately constructional difficulties did

Salisbury Cathedral: thirteenth-century craftsmen built the body of the cathedral; fourteenth-century craftsmen added the tower and magnificent steeple

not mar the beauty of the finished buildings. In the whole of Europe there is nothing more graceful than Salisbury spire, and the lofty arches, ribbed vaulting, and stone tracery of Ely's octagon, lit from above by the windows of the lantern, give

The Octagon and Lantern at Ely Cathedral, built in the first half of the fourteenth century to replace the central tower which collapsed

the impression not of massive strength but of delicate precision.

The mullions and transoms of the smaller windows and of the tall lancet windows, which were characteristic of much English building in the twelfth century, had to be built into the walls and gables as they were being constructed. The masons had to tie into the stone work the corbels to carry the floor joists, the responds and springers for the arches and vaulting, the wall-plates to support the roof timbers, and the skeleton of the elaborate stone tracery, which became so popular for east windows after Henry III had rebuilt Westminster Abbey. Then there remained only the internal pillars and arches to be built before the carpenters could begin work on the roof.

Most English roofs were made of oak. Their principal framework consisted of pairs of rafters coupled together in inverted Vs, and held at the apex by a ridge pole, itself supported on uprights based on the wall-plates or tie-beams. This basic construction was strengthened by braces, purlins, and collars. A large building, such as an abbey church or a palace, required three or four roofs to span its total width. The middle roof rested entirely on the pillars and arches which divided the interior of the building. Limitations imposed by the maximum possible roof span strictly controlled the design of Norman buildings, but later in the Middle Ages carpenters became more skilful and daring, and were able to construct roofs over sixty feet wide. Across the rafters they pegged or nailed laths, and on the laths the slaters hung overlapping blue slates, thin stone flags, or tiles, much as they do today. As miners from Cumberland to the Mendips steadily increased the supply of lead, more master masons ordered lead for roof-covering as well as for gutters. Normally the rain water which fell on the roof was allowed to spout to the ground through the mouths of over-hanging gargoyles, but in the later Middle Ages lead down-pipes were often used to bring the water to earth more conveniently if less spectacularly.

In the fourteenth and fifteenth centuries, roofs were made to add to the beauty of the finished building. The masons developed rib vaulting and then fan and lierne vaulting to cover the inside of the roofs with decorated stone. This work can be seen at its best in such buildings as the Divinity Schools at Oxford, St. George's Chapel, Windsor, and the many-sided chapter-houses which became such a feature of English cathedrals. The carpenters, who had no wish to hide the roof timbers, invented the hammer-beam roof, which permitted a wider, flatter span, and could be decorated with wooden carvings or heraldic shields painted upon the hammer beams and ceiling panels. The roofs of Westminster Hall

The timber roof of Necton church, Norfolk

and a number of East Anglian churches show how effectively this type of roof could be constructed and adorned.

DECORATORS

Once the roof was on, the masons and the carpenters had done their main work. They still had to finish the stone tracery in the most elaborate window-spaces, cut the decoration on the capitals and arches, assemble the prefabricated stonework,

Carpenters at work: squaring timbers

hang the doors, and set up the screen and choir stalls which had been carved in the carpenters' workshop. But other workmen, principally the plasterers, tilers, glaziers, and painters, could now begin their respective tasks. If the owners could afford to improve upon the utility rush-covered earth flooring, tilers were needed to lay a floor of tiles or marble blocks. They learned to use these materials decoratively. They arranged them in geometrical patterns. They interspersed thin coloured strips of stone between the marble blocks, or set white pipe-clay designs into channels which had been pressed into the clay tiles before firing. For particularly important jobs they used glazed decorated tiles in various colours, chiefly greens and yellows.

Throughout the Middle Ages builders tended to regard a good floor as an expensive luxury, but from the end of the twelfth century they gradually accepted that window-glazing, expensive though it was, must be considered a necessity for churches and other major buildings. In the fourteenth and fifteenth centuries English white glass cost about 4d. or 5d. a square foot, but the coveted stained glass cost at least three times and often over six times that price. Much of this extra cost came from the need to

Carpenters at work: sawing planks

transport the basic coloured glass from Normandy or the Rhineland, because English glass-makers could not manufacture

Fan-vaulting at Sherborne Abbey, Dorset. Late fifteenth-century work

coloured glass at competitive prices until the latter half of the fifteenth century. The Weald was one of the most important manufacturing centres for white glass, and both London and York had celebrated gilds of glaziers. The medieval glassmaker melted his metal in small iron pots, and had difficulty in producing pieces which were uniform in thickness or much bigger in area than a square foot. To colour the glass he added metallic oxides to the molten mixture. Silver oxide gave him yellow glass, iron compounds different shades of green, copper compounds either blue-green or ruby, and the vagaries of chance

The hammer-beam roof of Westminster Hall, constructed at the end of the fourteenth century

unexpected colours, often treasured beyond all others. Pure white glass was rare: most mixes produced a yellow or blue tinge, which the glassmaker could not eradicate, but could increase in intensity by reheating. The artist painted the design on the pieces of coloured glass with paints made from a mixture of ground copper and glass, or, in the later Middle Ages, from various metallic oxides mixed with gum arabic and vinegar. Later artists sometimes covered the pieces of glass with a wash of paint, and then scratched their design on the dried surface. If the basic glass were white or lightly-coloured, this technique allowed more light to enter the building, and the resulting two-colour design made a pleasant contrast from the neighbouring multi-coloured windows. York Minster, whose fourteenth- and fifteenth-century glass made in nearby Stonegate escaped both Puritan and Nazi destruction, has some splendid examples of this work, notably in the Bell-Founders' Window and the long lancets of the far-famed Five Sisters' Window.

The elaborately carved choir stalls at Chester Cathedral. Late fourteenth-century work

When the artist had finished his work by whatever process he wished, the glazier then fused the paint into the surface of the glass by reheating and slowly cooling the glass again in an annealing furnace. The many pieces which formed the window had then to be fitted together jig-saw wise on a table, and each piece fastened to its neighbours by strips of lead soldered together and folded over the edges of the glass. Finally, more strips of lead secured the finished window to the iron saddle-bars, which the masons had previously tied into the stone work of the window spaces.

Colour, bright, metallic, and, if possible, gleaming, delighted the unsophisticated eye of the Middle Ages. In favourable areas freeholders grew woad, madder, weld, and safflower, and merchants bought from Venetian traders brazilwood and indigo in order that the dyers could produce blue, yellow, and various shades of red cloth. Coloured hangings enlivened churches as did the clothes of any aristocratic worshippers, for both men and women dressed colourfully if they could afford to do so. In Norman times fashionable noblemen wore cloaks with material and lining of contrasting colours, and at Richard II's court parti-coloured hose, dagges, and tippets, and the choice of primary colours for tunic, cloak, hat, and decorative adornments helped the gentlemen to outshine and outglitter the ladies. The dyers, exercising their semi-secret art, tried with varied success to mix the primary colours into

Tile designs from Great Malvern Priory

Extravagant fashions worn by the wealthy in the late Middle Ages

greens, oranges, and purples. They used alum to fix the colours more permanently on the woollen or flax fibres, but it required skill and good fortune to avoid dull and patchy dyeing. The medieval potter was just as anxious as the dyer to achieve a range of brilliant colours. He experimented with iron and copper salts to turn his lead glazing yellow, orange, and green, but his colours remained cloudy and unsatisfactory. Not until the sixteenth century did English kilns produce brighter and more varied colours. The painted and lustre pottery, which rich householders prized so highly in the later Middle Ages, had to be imported from southern Europe and the Near East. Limited in range though they were, metallic paints undoubtedly gave the people of the Middle Ages their most satisfactory colours, and the desired sparkle and gleam had to come from a display of jewels or from gold and silver used in the form of lace, thread, or personal ornament which only the rich could afford. Columns, statues, bosses, corbels, hammer-beams, and decorative ironwork, all were gilded, silvered, or painted in bright red, blue, or yellow. Tempera paintings covered the plastered walls and the wooden panels of screens, altar, or backs of chairs, which had been suitably prepared beforehand by covering the wood first with linen and then with a thin surface of plaster of Paris. The artists mixed their powdered colours with size, the white of eggs, or even with honey. In the fourteenth and fifteenth centuries they would probably use oil for important work. The most common colours in the twelfth century were red, yellow, and black painted on the white background, but later artists often coloured the background, and managed to introduce blue, green, grey, and occasionally purple into their range of colours.

The medieval churches which can be visited today are not seen, therefore, as they were five hundred years ago. Apart from the stained glass they are far more sober in appearance, for the twentieth century, almost as much as the nineteenth, tends to condemn medieval decoration as garish and tasteless, and to look upon the shining, clashing colours as profaning the beauty achieved by the carpenter's and master-mason's use of line and pattern. It is very doubtful if any medieval carpenter or mason could have been found to accept this view, for he, like all his contemporaries, would probably have considered a large building, secular or ecclesiastical, to have been incomplete and dull without plenty of bright colour. By the last century of the Middle Ages church decoration had become a highly organised business. Greater national wealth was allowing such new patrons as the wool merchants of the Cotswolds, the cloth manufacturers of East Anglia, and the richer town gilds to pay for carvers, glaziers, and painters to decorate parish churches in a style previously restricted to cathedrals and monasteries. To supply this new demand, groups of craftsmen, usually centred on a large town, ac-

Dyers at work

cepted commissions, and, like the masons, lived on the site until the work was done. Not unnaturally they tended to work in small teams, repeat favourite designs, and develop labour-saving tricks of the trade, so that their craftsmanship was usually competent but rarely original or inspired.

ILLUMINATORS AND PRINTERS

The earl of Warwick in Shaw's *St. Joan* complained that

The potter at his wheel

"nowadays", which was 1429, "instead of looking at books, people read them". He professed himself content to turn over the pages and admire the "rich black writing in beautiful borders, and illuminated pictures cunningly inset". Warwick belonged to the medieval majority, because for every one who used a book for serious reading and study in the Middle Ages, there must have been a score or more who ignored the text and admired the design, the lettering, the colour, and the pictures. Each book represented hours of patient labour by many craftsmen. The skinner and the parchment-maker combined to produce from sheep or calf skins the parchment or vellum. The scribe wrote in ink with a goose quill, and the illuminator worked with gold- and silver-leaf laid upon a thin foundation of plaster of Paris, and with paints similar to those used by the glass painters. The surface of the parchment took ink and paint well, but the exactness of the lettering and the complexity of design in most of the surviving manuscripts speak eloquently of the technique and patience of the scribes and illuminators. When the writing was finished, the sheets of parchment were stitched together and bound in wooden boards covered with good quality leather decorated with gold-leaf designs. Obviously books made with such an expenditure of labour and material were scarce. The churches took great pride in their illuminated Bibles, psalters, and service books, and the colleges chained to the cases in their libraries their Latin translations of Greek and Arabic authors. Only under supervision and in hours of daylight did they allow students to read them. When scribes became more numerous in the fourteenth and fifteenth centuries, determined scholars found it possible to acquire a few plain texts of their own. Chaucer's clerk of Oxenford spent the little money he had on books, so that there were

144

at his beddes heed
Twenty bokes, clad in blak or reed,
Of Aristotle and his philosophye.

But to the end of the Middle Ages none but the richest could afford to purchase private copies of fully illuminated, bound books.

The style and fashion of illumination varied considerably during the Middle Ages. The English tradition was impressionistic. With a sparing use of bright colour and an economy of line worthy of Fougasse, English artists of the tenth and eleventh centuries sketched and suggested their lively figures. The Normans preferred heavier, more solid drawing, and a plentiful use of colour. They elaborated the initial letters of each chapter with human and animal figures, and decorated the margins of each page with patterned scrolls or stiffly-posed animals, some purely mythical like the dragons and phoenix, others heard of but not seen like the elephants drawn with ears erect or the crocodiles armed with cow's horns. The large Bibles written in the twelfth century by the scribes of the chief

A fifteenth-century book of hours. The picture, the initial letters, and the scroll work are all in bright colours

monastic houses contain the best work of this Romanesque school of art. Despite the widespread use of abbreviations, each transcription filled two or three heavy volumes generously illustrated with designs and drawings. Most of the pictures represented Biblical scenes, but they were invariably peopled by men and women wearing medieval dress and using medieval tools, just as today Western European pictures of Christ still

Chained books in Merton College Library, Oxford

show the influence of Italian Renaissance painters, and Biblical pictures drawn by Chinese and Negro artists often portray Christ and His apostles as mongolian or negroid. Thirteenth-century artists were fond of painting moral, allegorical pictures. In the De Quincey Apocalypse, now in Lambeth Palace Library, a penitent woman is shown using a shield inscribed with the names of the Trinity to ward off arrows shot at her by the devil, depicted, as was usual, as a grotesque with human limbs, webbed feet, tail, and horns. Over the penitent's head one angel whisks away the flies of evil thoughts, and another holds the sword of judgment. Beneath her foot a snake writhes, and from the top of the tree which represents the world, a cock, symbolising a preacher, crows to the empty heavens. To complicate the picture further a peasant is hacking at the base of the tree, and a bird, perched on the penitent's chair, is either encouraging her in her defiance of the devil or trying to distract her attention. A good friar would have no difficulty in using this picture for half-a-dozen powerful

The allegorical picture from the De Quincey Apocalypse, to which reference is made on this page

sermons. Compared with such complicated allegories, favourite Victorian moral pictures, such as Poynter's "Faithful unto Death" or Watt's "Mammon", seem to do no more than shout simple slogans.

Style changed again, from the Romanesque to the Gothic, during the middle decades of the thirteenth century. Delicacy of drawing and daintiness of lettering became the new ideals. The whole of the Bible, illuminated with neat initials in blue and gold and slender decorated margins, could now be enclosed within the boards of a single volume. The artists experimented with colour, employing glass-painting techniques such as colour-washing the background of the picture and using ink to outline the figures. They strove for more natural poses, but they did not succeed in putting their figures into much better perspective or giving them shadows. Matthew Paris, the St.

147

Albans monk who was illuminator and goldsmith as well as historian, showed what beautiful work could be done by black and white drawing merely tinted with colour. He influenced other artists in St. Albans and London, but before the end of the thirteenth century profusion of colour and ornament was back in fashion, and pages again had elaborate borders decorated with leaves, birds, animals, grotesques, and heraldic medallions. Illumination was no longer a monopoly of the monks, and the subject matter of pictures not so strictly religious as it had been. Both Henry III and Edward I employed lay scribes and

An early printing press

artists, and during their reigns laymen began to work alongside monks in the *scriptoria* of monastic houses.

The fifteenth century witnessed the biggest changes. The craft of manufacturing paper first came to Italy and Spain from the Islamic countries at the end of the thirteenth century, but another hundred years passed before paper was being made north of the Alps. English merchants began importing it from France, Italy, and the Holy Roman Empire in the early years of the fifteenth century. Paper cheapened book production, and scriveners cheapened it further by using wooden blocks for picture printing. Carvers prepared the blocks, the designs of which were often copied from manuscript drawings, and the scriveners covered them with a thin ink, and then pressed damp paper on them to take off impressions of the outline picture.

148

This method allowed only one side of the paper to be used, but that was sufficient for book illustrations, for pictures and texts in pamphlet form, or for the playing cards which were rapidly becoming a popular pastime in England. Some block-prints were designed to be coloured by hand, but fashion once again began to favour uncoloured or tinted illustrations. Many black and white pictures drawn by English artists in the fifteenth century show realism and perspective comparable with that which was being achieved by the early Renaissance artists on the continent.

The concluding paragraph from Dictes or Sayengis of the Philosophers, *printed by Caxton in 1477*

The block-picture and the block-page led directly to printing with movable type. William Caxton, who had already printed a book in English in Bruges, set up the first English press at Westminster in 1476. He published *Dictes or Sayengis of the Philosophers* in 1477, and before his death fifteen years later printed almost one hundred different titles. Three or four other presses quickly followed in London, and both Oxford and St. Albans had printers of their own for most of the 'eighties. All these presses used wooden type. One craftsman inked the assembled type, and his colleague pressed each sheet of paper as evenly as he could upon it. The process was slow, but it produced good quality printing and quickened the production of books beyond all medieval dreams. Missals, breviaries, and books of hours, grammars, tracts, and law books, copies of Chaucer, Malory, and Langland, all began to be available to anyone who could pay a few pence, and from continental book-sellers English merchants were importing clearly-printed copies of the Vulgate, and of new editions of Latin and Greek texts. An academic and educational revolution had begun.

Further Reading

L. F. Salzman, *Building in England down to 1540.*
D. Knoop and G. P. Jones, *The Medieval Mason.*
R. F. Swartwout, *The Monastic Craftsman.*
O. E. Saunders, *English Art in the Middle Ages.*
— — *English Illumination.*
J. Harvey, *Gothic England.*
Joan Evans, *English Art, 1307-1461.*

VIII

Decay and Transition

Feudalism made war inevitable. All important land-holders paid rent either in the form of armed soldiers or in money which kings and barons promptly used for hiring mercenaries, and throughout Europe the nobly-born accepted fighting and campaigning as their inevitable and natural destiny. Many medieval writers deplored the disastrous results of war, but they did not condemn it as morally wrong. Honoré Bonet, a French contemporary of Chaucer, argued from many examples taken from the *Old Testament* and ancient history that war was natural to mankind. "We must understand", he wrote in *The Tree of Battles*, "that war comes from God, and not merely that He permits war, but that He has ordained it". Medieval war, however, was not waged between nation states on the pattern that has prevailed in Europe during the last three or four hundred years. Far more was it a conflict between the personal followers and vassals of the disputing kings or noblemen. "The first and principal thing", Bonet continued, "is that good knights should keep the oath which they have made to their lord to whom they belong . . . for the defence of his land". Therefore, personal differences, such as those between duke William and earl Harold or Edward I and Robert Bruce, could not help but end in war. Honour allowed neither compromise nor diplomatic acceptance of an adverse verdict, and both king and baron kept his personal troops ever ready to march against his enemies. Almost all the men-at-arms and footsoldiers who went with Coeur de Lion to Palestine or fought with Edward II at Bannockburn had been born in England, but they obeyed the call to arms not so much

ST. MARY'S TRAINING COLLEGE
BELFAST.

because they were Englishmen—they would have given that word very little of its modern significance—as because they had entered into a money contract with the king or were obliged by feudal oath to support him. Occasionally, honour required noblemen, as well as hired soldiers, to fight against the king of the land in which they were born. Their contemporaries did not automatically dub them traitors, because they accepted that the strongest of the bonds that held men together was vassalage and not patriotism.

The word *foreigner* had little meaning in the Middle Ages. Lanfranc and Anselm were not *foreign* archbishops to the people of eleventh-century England, and such assertive kings as Henry II and Edward I felt no humiliation when they paid homage to the French king for land they held in France. The *nations* were not at war when the vassals and hired soldiers of Edward III fought the vassals and hired soldiers of Philip of France at Crécy. Most of the overtones of nationalism were missing. Therefore it is unhistoric to project back into the Middle Ages later concepts of national pride and hatred of the foreigner. Shakespeare is a most notorious offender. King John's "no Italian priest shall tithe or toll in our dominions", or Gaunt's "this blessed plot, this earth, this realm, this England" are Elizabethan, not medieval, sentiments. The real Henry V would not have understood the implications of "upon one pair of English legs did march three Frenchmen". He never thought of himself as a Welshman, as the stage Henry does. Nor did he think that among his soldiers there was none "so mean and base that hath not noble lustre in his eyes"; for, like all other medieval people, King Henry thought of Europeans as divided into nobles, freemen, and peasants, rather than into Englishmen, Frenchmen, and Burgundians. He was contemptuous of ordinary mortals, and would have been as indignant as Shaw's earl of Warwick if he had heard his soldiers calling themselves *Englishmen*, as if England was *their* country and, by implication, not *his*.

Considerably less than two centuries after the battle of Agincourt the Spanish Armada was threatening the invasion of England. Queen Elizabeth reviewed her troops at Tilbury, and declared that she came to "her loving people" at that time "not for my recreation and disport, but being resolved in the midst and heat of the battle, to live or die amongst you all, to lay down for my God, and for my kingdom, and for my people, my honour and my blood, even in the dust". Unlike many medieval monarchs, Elizabeth was not finding "quarrel in a straw". Still less was she looking for ransoms. She was voicing England's

English troops embarking for France during the Hundred Years War

defiance of powerful Spain. However much she might insist that she alone should direct foreign policy, there is no doubt that at Tilbury she was speaking not only for herself, but also for her nobles, the middle classes, the townsmen, the yeomen, and those of the landless peasantry who, downtrodden and harried by the law as they were, considered themselves members of a closely-knit community. *The Queen* had become a rallying cry not for her vassals, but for her fellow-countrymen.

Such fundamental changes of outlook grow slowly in human

societies, and the roots of this strong and unified national fervour of the Elizabethan age can be easily traced through a tangle of medievalism into the fifteenth century, and less surely into the fourteenth. When the Hundred Years War began in 1340, Edward III, in traditional fashion, laid claim to the French throne, and called upon his vassals to help him fight for his honour. The early campaigns, which included the battles of Crécy and Poitiers, were fought in the spirit of medieval chivalry. Men-at-arms on both sides mutually acknowledged

The old and the new in fifteenth-century warfare

the valour of their opponents, and recognised that honour and duty compelled both friend and foe to fight as resolutely as possible. But as the war dragged on into the reign of Richard II and into the fifteenth century, a different kind of hostility appeared, especially among the lower ranks. The growing contemptuous hatred for the French in the heart of the English soldier was balanced by the Frenchman's increasing determination to drive the foreign devils out of *his* country; so that the last stages of the long struggle displayed as many characteristics of future national wars as they did of traditional feudal wars. On the French side, Joan of Arc personified the new outlook. Her belief that God never intended the English 'goddams' to leave their own country to trespass in France was older than she, but her death gave it new life. So strongly did it grow that the French chronicler, Basin, writing towards the end of the war, could strike a very modern propaganda note with, "In the opinion of many, the English are not human beings and men, but senseless and ferocious beasts which go about to devour people". On the English side, the London merchants and shopkeepers, who for many years had detested all overseas traders living in their town, began to direct their hostility particularly against the French. Louis XI's blandishments and offers of advantageous fairs in Normandy failed to lure them from their preference for Burgundy. Burgundy could be very exasperating, but Londoners believed her to be their natural ally against the common enemy, France. To them and to many others in the middle decades of the fifteenth century it was clear that the country in which a man was born could not help but determine his outlook and his feelings. They recognised that western Europeans were divided into national groups as naturally as they were divided into social groups. Before the end of the century it was widely held that the national were stronger than the social divisions.

These new views eventually modified the policy of the crown. Edward IV and Henry VII claimed the French throne as loudly as Henry V had done, but medieval conceptions of honour did not prevent the one from making the profitable Treaty of Picquigny before he had struck a blow at Louis XI's forces, nor the other from accepting Charles VIII's offer of a favourable financial settlement at Etaples. They both preferred inglorious success to ruinous victory. Edward I and Henry V would have described these treaties as dishonourable and craven: Edward IV and Henry VII saw them as common-sense and statesmanlike settlements. The outlook and methods of diplomacy were obviously changing fundamentally. A few discerning observers might already have caught glimpses of the full-blooded national-ism ahead.

This slowly-evolving awareness of the entity of England was one of the main characteristics of the period of transition from medieval to modern times. It seeped into the consciousness of men, and gradually transformed their way of looking at things. But it was not the only characteristic, nor the only force at work. Economic factors, equally powerful, were also accelerating the change.

THE BLACK DEATH

In the autumn of 1348, two short years after Edward III's soldiers had triumphantly defeated the armies of the French and Scottish kings at Crécy and Neville's Cross, the Black Death arrived in Hampshire and Dorset. Men had dreaded its coming for many weeks. Laggard, incomplete, but numerous reports had informed them of an exceptionally rabid pestilence, which in the spring had reaped a heavy human harvest in Italy, Spain, and Southern France. By high summer it was known to be in Paris and Normandy, carrying off with complete impartiality victorious and pleasure-seeking English soldiers and depressed French peasants. Longbow and lance offered no protection against this unseen enemy, whose strength increased every month. Special prayers, solemn processions, and widespread repentance did not keep it out of England. It rampaged westward to Devon, Cornwall, Somerset, and Bristol, northward to Oxfordshire, and eastward through Sussex and Surrey. It reached London in October, and for the next ten months ravaged its way through the narrow streets and stinking alleys of the poor, and the large gardens and lofty halls of the rich. The well-nourished stood the best chance of survival, but no one was immune, and nowhere offered safety and refuge. Bradwardine, the newly-ordained, scholarly archbishop of Canterbury, lasted two days in London before the plague killed him. Westminster Abbey lost its abbot and twenty-six monks: scores of lesser folk died every day. New burial grounds had to be hastily opened. The bishop of London hallowed ground called *Normannes lond*, and Sir Walter Manny bought land for a cemetery at

The reception ward in a fourteenth-century hospital

Smithfield, outside the city boundaries. Five thousand plague victims were buried with scant ceremony at Smithfield during the first twelve months. In the worst period the daily rate of burial at this one place alone touched two hundred.

From London the plague passed rapidly into the rich East Anglian villages and towns, across the open fields of the Midlands to the small and scattered hamlets of Wales and the northern counties.

A ward in a fifteenth-century hospital

> *Nature came after   with many keen sores.*
> *Pocks and pestilence,   and slew much people*
> *Death drove down after him   and pashed all to dust.*

The only wry consolation in the north was that a Scottish army, apparently convinced, like Langland's Reason, that the Black Death was a just punishment for the "pure sin" of the English, assembled near Selkirk to profit from God's timely intervention, only to be stricken and dispersed by plague before it could begin to march south.

The Black Death took the best part of three years to spend itself. Familiar as medieval Europe was to accepting deadly

Out-door relief

infections as one of the normal hazards of human life, it regarded this attack as unprecedently severe. The disease struck viciously, and, with frightening if merciful speed, within a few hours reduced young and healthy men and women into pock-marked corpses. It took two forms—painful abscesses which stronger patients might survive with careful lancing, and an incurable rash of black pustules all over the body. Medieval medicine stood helpless. Many people appreciated that crowded towns were more vulnerable than scattered farmsteads: many believed that foul smells carried infection. The king prorogued Parliament indefinitely. Those few burgesses who had some where to go moved into the countryside, and unwittingly helped to spread the pestilence. So general was the fear of contact with the afflicted that many victims must have died unnecessarily of neglect.

Plague is a general term used until less than a century ago to cover a variety of infectious diseases from bubonic and pneumonic plague, through typhus and typhoid fever, to virulent forms of 'sweating sickness' and influenza. The most devastating of all the plagues are bubonic and pneumonic, and the Black Death was either one of these or a combination of the two. The disease first affected black rats, from which fleas transferred the infection to human beings. Once the plague was under way, it had no need for rats or fleas to spread it; and the only effective treatment, which was careful nursing to preserve the patient's strength, did not appear among medieval remedies. To repent by fasting, or to remove unwholesome humours by bleeding, made the body weaker and more likely to succumb. More than one million men, women, and children, over one-third of the total population, died in England between 1348 and 1351, and many of those who survived fell victims to subsequent lesser outbreaks in 1356, 1361–1362, and 1368–9. The 'pestilence that walketh in the darkness' and 'the sickness that destroyeth in the noonday' had truly caused a thousand to fall beside them and ten thousand at their right hand. They could hear the Psalmist with understanding; and, more than any other generation of Englishmen, they would readily have appreciated the anguish and helplessness of those Japanese who lived through the terror of Nagasaki and Hiroshima.

ECONOMIC AND POLITICAL CONSEQUENCES OF THE BLACK DEATH

Two hundred years before the Black Death, England had begun to enjoy a trade boom. Despite the exceptional attention given by abbots and earls to the more economic use of land, the supply of grain, meat, and especially wool could not keep pace with the demand from home and foreign markets. Population increased, yet labour remained scarce and valuable. Some land-holders, eager to grow and sell more produce, exacted extra duties from their villeins and cottars. Others, anxious not to lose efficiency by struggling to farm their bigger demesne lands with the unwilling labour of aggrieved men, preferred to sell their villeins their freedom for a rent, and use the cash to hire more controllable labour. The gap between the living standards of bondmen and freemen, and of successful and unsuccessful farmers noticeably widened.

Early in the fourteenth century the inevitable slump followed. Foreign demand for wool slackened and then began to diminish, because European buyers, themselves affected by the fall-off in trade, could not so easily afford the high prices required by English merchants, who were struggling against the handicap of heavy export duties. Land-holders began to curtail production and reduce costs. Many who had freed their villeins tried to recapture their services, because villein-labour was cheaper than hired labour: others, who were desperate for money, rented surplus demesne land to villagers. Expediency prompted these contradictory actions. Every man who was free enough to manoeuvre judged the situation for himself, and tried to squeeze from it all he could. Some judged wisely, others did not.

War, first against Scotland and then against France, seemed

to offer a way out of the slump. It drained off a little surplus labour and stimulated the demand for food and clothing, but in the end its general waste and need of taxes damaged the economy more than it helped it. A far more useful and healthy development was the surprising growth of the English cloth trade. To compensate for the dwindling demand for wool, Merchant Adventurer companies belonging chiefly to London,

Ingarsby, Leicestershire: one of the many villages which the economic changes of the later Middle Ages forced its inhabitants to desert

York, Ipswich, and Bristol, looked for other English goods to sell abroad. They found that, thanks to the cheapness of wool in England compared with the cost of English wool abroad, they could sell English cloth without difficulty from Scandinavia to Italy. Very shortly they had orders for more cloth than English looms could weave. It was not that wool was in short supply; on the contrary, the timely expansion of the cloth trade had saved most wool-growers from ruin. It was that gild-merchant and craft-gild restrictions on the development of weaving were causing a production bottle-neck and threatening the trade with unnecessarily high prices. To surmount these difficulties, merchants turned for help to hundreds of part-time cottage spinners, weavers, fullers, and dyers, who lived outside the towns and were not controlled by a gild. This new policy began as a rescue operation, but cottage textile-workers steadily became the chief source of supply and the most important group in the industry. The villages of East Anglia, the Cotswolds, and south-western counties grew rich with cloth-making in the fifteenth century, and when John Leland visited northern England in 1540 he commented upon the activity in spinning and weaving in the villages of Bradford, Halifax, and Bolton. Manchester, which already had a reputation for woollen textiles known as "Manchester cottons", had grown so prosperous out of the new industry that Leland described it as "the fairest, best buildid, quikkest, and most populus tounne of al Lancastreshire".

Before the cloth industry had developed sufficiently to counter-act the slump, the Black Death began to ravage its way through the country. It jolted the economic cart so violently that it rattled along the ruts of change faster than it had ever done since the English first colonised Britain. Together with the subsequent outbreaks, the plague drastically reduced the labour force. There had been a surplus of labour before the Black Death, but during the second half of the fourteenth century hundreds of land-holders were eventually forced to abandon much of the land, which they had struggled to keep in cultivation. In 1351 the king's government, through the Statute of Labourers, ruled that rents and rates of wages should be fixed in order to prevent men from exploiting the scarcity of labour, but the very fact that successive governments reissued the act in 1357, 1361, and several times in the fifteenth century is proof enough that this legislative remedy failed to cure so fundamental an economic illness. All labourers naturally resented measures to keep down wages. But also many hirers of labour, including royal bailiffs and rich ecclesiastics, ignored the statute by offering competi-tive wages, and by not enquiring whether their newly-hired

161

ST. MARY'S TRAINING COLLEGE
BELFAST.

*"When Adam delved, and Eve span,
Who was then a gentleman?"*
This was the theme of John Ball's political
sermons in 1381

workmen were freemen, who had the right to move to new employment, or villeins, who had escaped from bondage. Other land-holders tried to solve their problems by leasing demesne land or deserted open fields to peasant families at a nominal rent. Others grassed their plough-lands and concentrated upon breeding sheep and cattle. The foreign demand for English cloth was keeping the wool market reasonably steady, and per acre sheep absorbed less labour than oats or barley.

A completely depressed peasantry is not rebellious, but an awakening peasantry, disappointed and prevented by changed circumstances from continuing its emancipation, quickly becomes restless and dangerous. Impelled by the sense of righting past wrongs and impatient of any other reasoning but the frustration in their people's hearts, its leaders tend to push forward towards their vision of what is possible for them and their fellows. Significantly, John Ball and Wat Tyler came from south-eastern England, which had benefited in full measure from the prosperous days of the boom. Thousands of peasants in Essex and Kent resented seeing their new standards of living slipping away because they were being compelled to return to labour services, while their more fortunate fellows, often employed on neighbouring estates, seemed to be enjoying more independence than ever. They listened eagerly to Ball's political sermons, and in 1381, stung into righteous anger by French attacks upon coastal towns and by the imposition of the poll tax, they followed the lead of Wat Tyler, and rose in armed revolt against everyone and every condition which seemed to be making their lives miserable.

Like Jack Cade's Rebellion in 1450, which had the support of many well-to-do as well as poor people, the Peasants' Revolt was provoked by war-exhaustion and economic change. Both risings expressed widespread bewilderment and turbulence of mind. They neither solved any problems nor increased the pace of the uncomfortable change from feudalism to capitalism. And both were followed by heavy retribution. In 1381 the peasants returned from London to their holdings in Essex and Kent with Richard II's promises ringing in their ears and the sounds of victory in their voices. But once they were safely dispersed, soldiers arrived to burn down their houses and execute their leaders, and a very different Richard from the one with whom they had parleyed at Mile End declared uncompromisingly at Waltham, "Villeins you were and villeins you are; in bondage you shall abide". Cade's triumph was equally short-lived. Within a week of leaving London with full pardon he had been hunted down and killed in Sussex, and at Canterbury and other centres his lieutenants were then arraigned before the gentle Henry VI and condemned to death. Among the rebels on both occasions were men with different interests and problems, and with varied dreams of the society they wished to see in being. They were not a political group pursuing a policy and plan for reform. They were expressing a real but ill-defined resentment, which they all felt against the social conditions in which they lived. Villeinage gradually died out, but its disappearance did not automatically ensure prosperity. Money rents had to be earned by hard work before they could be paid, and both the

The death-bed of a rich man in the late Middle Ages

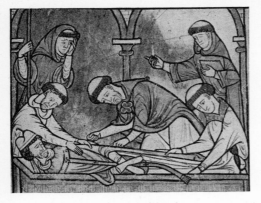

Laying a distinguished brother to rest

demands of successive kings for fighting funds and the recurrent need in the fifteenth century to buy armed protection or bribe away threatened pillage and theft prevented men from feeling safe or growing prosperous. The merchants and craftsmen in the towns and the smaller land-holders and yeoman farmers in the countryside all looked to the crown to curb the power of the barons, to discipline the ex-soldiers and landless poor, and allow commerce, industry, and farming to develop in peace and security. Both Edward IV and Richard III appreciated the gravity of the problem, and took steps to strengthen the central administration and make royal justice effective. Henry VII achieved greater success by restraining the "over-mighty subject", encouraging overseas trade, maintaining peace, and increasing the wealth and authority of the crown. But not even he could control the effects of inflation, or prevent a renewed European demand for English wool from causing more en-closures for sheep rearing, more evictions from arable land, and consequently a larger army of "sturdy beggars" seeking employment.

END AND BEGINNING

Although a century is an artificial division of time, it has seemed possible to detect in the last years of some centuries a widespread overthrowing of moral standards and a general atmosphere of boredom, pessimism, and resignation. That human spirits droop with the decline of a century may be more imagined than real: they are probably more naturally depressed when one epoch is passing into the next. It is not easy to say when the Middle Ages finally ceased to be; but, as we have seen, there is no doubt that the changes in English life which were to carry the country from the Middle Ages into the Modern Age were steadily gaining momentum during the second half of the fourteenth and the whole of the fifteenth century. And during those years of decline from the high hopes and activity of earlier times, the waking thoughts of thousands of men and women in England were haunted by death. It was not merely that popular preachers, poets, and artists in wood, stone, and paint repetitively emphasised that in the midst of life mankind constantly lives with death, but that they insisted on dwelling morbidly upon the decay of the body and on the worms that await its arrival in the grave. " At churche in the charnel churles aren evel

Heavy mourning at a funeral

[hard] to know", sang Langland, and went on to say that it is impossible to distinguish knight from knave when both are mouldering corpses. Later poets tended to dwell not on Langland's picture of death the equaliser, but upon the more ghoulish conception of death the destroyer of human dignity and the ultimate victor over mankind. Despite their profession of Christianity, their thoughts remained with the body and not with the soul.

> *Fowl and stinkande is mi roting*
> *On me, ihesu, thou have mercy!*

cried a late fourteenth-century poet; and in the following century many writers could not free themselves from the oppressive belief that the inevitable end of all men was to be "clad in claye".

This constant theme of vanished glories, usually expressed far less wistfully than Villon's *where are the snows of yesteryear?*, the popularity of the *danse macabre*, the fashion of placing on tombs stone skeletons instead of recumbent knights and ladies, the preference for graveyards as places to stroll in, all these aspects of late medieval life illustrate its preoccupation with death and putrescence. In large measure it was a legacy of the

165

Black Death and of the wretched twenty years that followed. Many men sought refuge in repentance and good works. The Carthusians persisted in their strict form of life, friars and secular priests preached repentance from their pulpits, and morality plays frequently stressed the redemptive power of Christ. Far more men, however, abandoned themselves to recklessness and indulgence. They tried to forget the horrors of

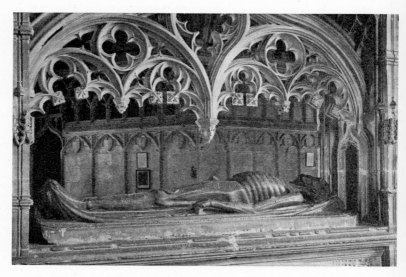

The Wakeman Effigy, Tewkesbury Abbey, Gloucestershire. The skeleton figure is a deliberate reminder of the inevitability of death

life and the hideousness of death in hours of drunkenness and frivolity.

Yet alongside this evidence of widespread loss of faith and no joy in living, there are signs of the new age ahead. Fresh reviving air is blowing into England from across the Channel. New ideals are firing the enthusiasm of a minority of scholars and teachers, exciting challenges are being thrown down in political and theological thought, art and architecture are changing fundamentally, technical skills are promising to raise the slowly-improving standards of living still further, and news of the widening world being discovered by Prince Henry the Navigator, Diaz, Vasco da Gama, and Columbus is opening up endless possibilities in the minds of the imaginative and adventurous. To the traditionalists the last years of the Middle Ages could not help but be depressing and disheartening, for to them it would seem as if the new generations were defacing and destroying the England they had inherited. But to the young in heart it must have been, as Wordsworth said of a later awakening, "bliss . . . in that dawn to be alive "; and to the fortunate minority who were young in years as well as in heart it could well have been "very heaven".

Further Reading

C. L. Kingsford, *Prejudice and Promise in Fifteenth-Century England.*
G. W. Coopland, *The Tree of Battles of Honoré Bonet.*
E. E. Power, *The Wool Trade in Medieval English History.*
R. R. Bolgar, *The Classical Heritage and its Beneficiaries.*
J. Huizinga, *The Waning of the Middle Ages.*
The Oxford History of England, Vol. 6.

Index